Life Below Stairs

Life Below Stairs

Domestic servants in England
from Victorian times

FRANK E. HUGGETT

CHARLES SCRIBNER'S SONS
NEW YORK

1 3 5 7 9 11 13 15 17 19 I/C 20 18 16 14 12 10 8 6 4 2

First published in 1977 by Book Club Associates.
Library of Congress Catalog Card Number 77–83231
ISBN 0–684–15513–3

Designed by Harold Bartram
Picture research by Jaqueline Spigel

Printed in Great Britain

Contents

Introduction

There had never been so many domestic servants, both indoors and out, as there were in the Victorian age. They were everywhere. Out in the streets a pair of liveried footmen, carefully matched for height and often wearing padded silk stockings to make their legs look more curvaceous, stood up erect behind a swaying coach, clinging tightly onto the straps which alone ensured their safety. Further on, a young lady's maid walked respectfully a few paces behind her mistress, social distinctions between them being emphasised by the maid's less voluminous crinoline and the plainness of her cloak and skirt. Deep down in the basement kitchens, countless red-faced cooks fretted over the copper stewpans on the huge, coal-fired ranges; while upstairs, in the drawing rooms, neat parlourmaids, wearing small white caps, starched aprons and trim, black, floor-length dresses offered cups of tea from heavy silver trays to afternoon visitors. There were many other categories of men and women servants, all of whom we shall encounter in the following pages: house stewards, butlers, grooms of the chambers, valets, 'tigers' and among the female servants, housekeepers of two different kinds, 'plain' and 'professed' cooks, maids-of-all-work, and, later on, tweenies and 'step-girls'.

The servant industry expanded as rapidly in the Victorian age of the private family and personal charity as the 'caring industry' has in the modern era of paid social work for the public sector. What distinguished the Victorian age, however, from all others that preceded it was the great increase in the number of women servants and their regimentation into a separate servant hierarchy with special characteristics and problems of its own.

Women were latecomers to domestic service. In the middle ages, noble households were controlled by men, who were usually of noble or gentle birth themselves, and there were relatively few women servants apart from the waiting gentle-women, the nurses and the ubiquitous laundress. Even menial tasks in kitchen and bedchamber, and most of the more complex, such as cooking, were performed by men: they washed up, they cleaned the floors, they served at table. By the seventeenth century many more officials, professional men and merchants employed servants, particularly women who were both cheaper and more tractable than men. Women servants became even more common in the eighteenth century. These maidservants, who were usually recruited locally, were often employed not only in the house but also behind the counter or in the farmyard or the dairy, where they were frequently joined in their appointed tasks by their mistresses from whom they were sometimes little distinguished in dress, education or interests. There was no shame in household work or domestic service then. Mrs Mary Delany, a gifted amateur artist and a member of the ancient Granville family, who frequented the country mansions of the aristocracy, had no hesitation in praising her younger sister Ann as an 'excellent housewife' who could 'raise paste, feed poultry, keep accounts.'[1]

Some young servants, particularly in the towns, were overworked, underpaid drudges, who had to find their own bed in any dark corner of the kitchen and who were often beaten or cuffed; but other maidservants in country towns and remote villages had a far more pleasant life, becoming household treasures as highly valued and as familiar as an heirloom which brings pleasure and a sense of security to its custodian. It was not unknown for women, such as Mrs Armison of Kempsey, Worcestershire, to spend a whole lifetime of service in the same family:

To the Memory of
Mrs Sarah Armison
who died the 27th of April
1817
Aged 88 Years
77 of which she passed in
the Service of the Family
of Mrs Bell
Justly and deservedly lamented
by them
for integrity, rectitude
of Conduct and Amiable
Disposition[2]

Similar gratitude—and devotion—is commemorated in blurred letters on many stained and weatherbeaten tombstones in quiet churchyards throughout the English countryside. The tradition persisted, almost unimpaired, in some households right through the nineteenth century, and even beyond; but it was to become increasingly uncommon.

Already, by the end of the eighteenth century, some farmers' wives, grown fat and rich on high prices for corn, had forsaken the cold dairy for the refurbished drawing room, adopting a new and more genteel role as the mistress of their growing staff of household servants. Most of them could not afford to employ male indoor servants, but for some gawky, rough-handed, local footboy, absurdly attired in a gaudy livery made by a tailor in the nearest town; but they could afford to pay a cook, a sewing maid, or a nursemaid nine or ten guineas a year, which was double the wages of the little maid-of-all-work whom they had previously employed.

The social pretensions of these *nouveaux riches* were satirised by James Gillray, the brilliant son of a Chelsea pensioner, in his cruel cartoon of fat Farmer Giles and his wife and their equally obese daughter displaying her musical skills to their assembled neighbours. Satire, however, did not bite very deep in the Victorian age when so many middle-class women wanted to prove that they were 'ladies' by keeping the largest possible staff of servants: an aspiration for respectability which was transferred

Gillray's cartoon of Farmer Giles, his wife and their daughter Betty.

by some parasitic process to some of their own female employees who liked to pretend that they were not just ordinary servants but ladies' maids. Once this status-based process had started, there was a self-perpetuating tendency for the size of household staffs to increase.

Mrs Mary Sherwood, the prolific but almost forgotten author of some three hundred books, tells a delightful tale of how Ezekiel Wellwood, an eighteenth-century Worcestershire shop-

9

keeper, became the increasingly harassed victim of this early Parkinson's law after he had married a former servant from the local big house. Both his marriage and his business prospered until they received a visit one Monday morning from his wife's friend from the big house, a lady's maid known as Miss Kitty, who was 'hanging upon the arm of the butler, and dressed in a flowered *négligé* with a fly cap, and a hat all puffed about with pea-green ribands.' When Miss Kitty saw Ezekiel's wife in her old working clothes slaving over the washtub, she scolded him severely for his meanness and flounced out of the shop. He felt so guilty that he engaged a local woman called Betty Crump to come in every week to do the washing.

For three months peace reigned in the house until Miss Kitty favoured them with another visit for Sunday afternoon tea, bringing with her in addition to the butler another uninvited woman guest. While Ezekiel's wife was out in the kitchen, Miss Kitty again 'read him a lecture' for not employing a maid so that his wife would not have to demean herself by taking the best china tea set out of the cupboard in the presence of other ladies. Ezekiel would have resisted this new demand, but on her next visit, a few weeks later, Miss Kitty rebuked him yet again on the grounds that his wife was 'falling away' through hard work since her marriage. Even though Ezekiel knew that his wife's distraught appearance was merely the result of a particularly painful attack of toothache, he succumbed and agreed to invite his fifteen-year-old niece, Margaret, to come over from Kidderminster to help in the house.

Margaret, however, was temperamentally unsuitable for service, being a gossiping, good-looking 'fluttering' kind of girl, and the main effect of her presence was to increase the size of the family wash so that yet another local girl called Molly Brien had to be engaged to do the ironing. A year or so later, Margaret fell ill and the doctor ordered her to have more rest and more exercise in the open air. As a result Ezekiel was forced to hire a maid-of-all-work to assist his niece Margaret.

The climax—and the final addition to his staff—came when poor Ezekiel heard his wife agreeing to employ a little boy to run messages. Suddenly he realised that the increase in the number of his household staff to five had not produced cleanliness and order in the house, but only a care-worn wife, a great diminution in his savings, and utter confusion. 'Eight o'clock and no breakfast! the wet clothes all about the kitchen! the coal-dust trod into the parlour! not a thing in its place! not a dry corner to sit in!' Taking his courage in both hands, he decided to dismiss all his staff, realising that 'by multiplying servants, I have only increased the sum of my household business, and, instead of diminishing, added to the trouble and fatigue of my wife.' His wife accepted his decision gladly and they lived happily ever after.[3]

But Ezekiel and his wife were exceptional and the number of women servants continued to multiply in the nineteenth century, producing a grotesque change in the individual lives of many women, and the relationships between them, particularly in London and the other expanding towns and cities. The growth of domestic service was one of the most socially important, and in many ways unfortunate, consequences of the industrial revolution. There had never been so many young girls and women who, even though they might be reluctant to enter service, were nevertheless desperate to do so. The opening of cotton mills in the closing years of the eighteenth century had robbed many country women—the traditional spinsters—of their chief occupation, leaving domestic service as the main alternative employment. At the same time, the number of potential mistresses in the middle classes had increased greatly as their husbands prospered through the expansion of trade, manufactures and the professions. But these were mistresses of a new and different kind. These 'ladies', who might once have helped their husbands in their work, had been made idle and redundant by the separation of the workplace and the home and the increasing introduction of machinery. The small business which had formerly been conducted from a couple of rooms in the house or from an adjoining shed, had been moved to a separate workshop or factory, where the wife's help was no longer needed. The increase in the husband's wealth made it unnecessary for the wife to work outside the home, even if she had wished to do so, and the ready supply of cheap female labour made it equally unnecessary for her to work within it.

If only there had been a stronger intellectual tradition among the middle classes, these women might have found some more personally profitable employment in thought and cultural pursuits; but there was not. Mrs Newton Crosland, the Victorian journalist and novelist, recalls going to a charity bazaar in 1833 where two little sealed packets were on sale labelled 'A Lady's Horror' and 'A Gentleman's Horror'. On opening her packet the lady found merely a piece of black paper, cut out in the shape of a stocking, and labelled 'blackleg', the current slang term for a swindler at cards; and the gentleman discovered a similar stocking-shaped piece of paper, coloured blue.[4] These new ladies of the nineteenth century were condemned to a life of regular, machine-like child-bearing; their 'pretty crafts for ladies'; the management of their maids who were put into uniform for the first time in the nineteenth century; their public practice of religion; and perhaps, sometimes, their private regrets for a wasted life. Most of them, however, accepted the passive and inferior role which had been thrust upon them without reluctance or complaint. As Mrs Sandford wrote in *Female Improvement,* published a year before Queen Victoria came to the throne: 'It is the privilege of women of the superior order to be provided for, served and protected by others; and any labour, therefore, which they undertake is chiefly voluntary.'[5]

Ladies did not soil their hands with household tasks. The number of female indoor servants increased at a fantastic rate in

Victorian times so that by 1891 of all females above the age of ten, roughly one in eight were in domestic service and of those between the ages of fifteen and twenty, the proportion was nearly one in three.[6] Ten years later, in 1901, the total number of women servants had fallen very slightly from 1,386,167 to 1,330,783 but this was still the largest working group, male or female, in England and Wales.[7]

The story of domestic servants from Victorian times is much more than a nostalgic slice of history, replete with amusing anecdote and curious detail, though it contains many of those. It is also concerned with the reworking of the social fabric into a new and tighter pattern whose strands still enmesh us to this very day. The use of cheap 'slaveys' to lay, light and replenish so many inefficient open fires helped to delay the improvement of English homes to such an extent that many families found it extravagantly voluptuous to install central-heating systems even though they had been common in American and Continental homes for many years. The employment of self-professed working-class cooks to prepare pseudo-French dishes in middle-class homes under the instructions of mistresses who usually had at best only a theoretical knowledge of those exotic culinary delights, produced an excessive dependence on expensive ingredients and a residual contempt for the real virtues of traditional English cookery. But the rise of the female domestic servant had even more important social effects. A whole century of service, snobbery and pretension, and the relegation of the woman to the home, delayed the wider education of both mistress and maid and resulted in a restriction of their interests. The excessive dependence of the middle-class lady upon others, both male and female, the increasing atrophy of her mind and sensibilities, the sublimation of her sexual impulses into religion, her want of some purposeful occupation often produced, in the words of one Victorian writer, 'sleepless nights and useless days' which became 'a serious drag on woman's usefulness and happiness'.[8] Most ladies found no other outlet for their repressed anger and their frustration than their children, and their maids. It was little wonder that Thackeray wrote in *Vanity Fair:* 'the greatest tyrants over women are women'.

The memories of the insults, deprivations and petty oppressions to which so many servants were subjected passed into the oral folklore of the working classes, where it helped in mainly private ways to sustain the dichotomy of 'them and us' which had so many expressive counterparts in the world of 'upstairs, downstairs'. As a result, service became equated in many women's minds with servitude and for converse reasons the word 'lady' has become a pejorative term so that, as one reluctant peeress has told me, she now finds herself actually whispering her rank to shop assistants. The history of domestic service in the last 150 years or so must be concerned with masters and retainers as well as mistresses and maids and at a deeper level probes into the fundamental role of women in society.

Big House

Although very few of the Victorian middle classes could ever hope to emulate the landed aristocracy, and, indeed, would have been gravely shocked in more ways than one if they had only known what really went on, upstairs and downstairs, in some of the big houses they so greatly admired, they took these peers of the realm as their exemplars in manners, customs and the management of their own households. Members of Victorian society—that narrow, but never entirely closed, circle of some ten thousand men and women—were still rich, insouciant and self-assured enough to live like lords and ladies and to mould their servants to their own eccentricities. Lord Melbourne, the Prime Minister and mentor of the young Queen Victoria, had a great dislike of carrying a watch; when he wanted to know the time he would just shout out to any passing servant. That rich, eccentric dilettante, William Beckford, refused to have any servants' bells in Fonthill except in one room which was used occasionally by his daughter, the Duchess of Hamilton. He made his servants crouch in low, narrow ante-rooms so that they could come running in at his command. When he travelled abroad he took his own French cook with him, mainly to make omelettes, and he also insisted on transporting his own bed. Although he rarely entertained, he sometimes ordered a magnificent dinner at Fonthill and had the table laid for twelve guests, with a dozen liveried footmen in attendance. He would then dine in solitude, eating only one course and sending back all the rest.

The eighth Earl of Bridgewater, a fellow of All Souls College, Oxford, and the rector of two parishes in Wiltshire which he administered by proxy, was reputed to give even more extraordinary dinner parties in the Parisian mansion where he spent most of his later years. He, too, had his table laid for twelve, with footmen in attendance, but his guests were his favourite dogs, dressed in men's and women's clothes, and with immaculate table napkins round their necks. He also used to send his dogs out for a ride in his carriage, attended by liveried flunkies. Another member of society, who was a keen student of phrenology, was in the habit of running his hands over the face and heads of prospective servants before engaging them. Aristocratic eccentricities were not confined to men. The widow of Lord Cardigan, who led the Charge of the Light Brigade in

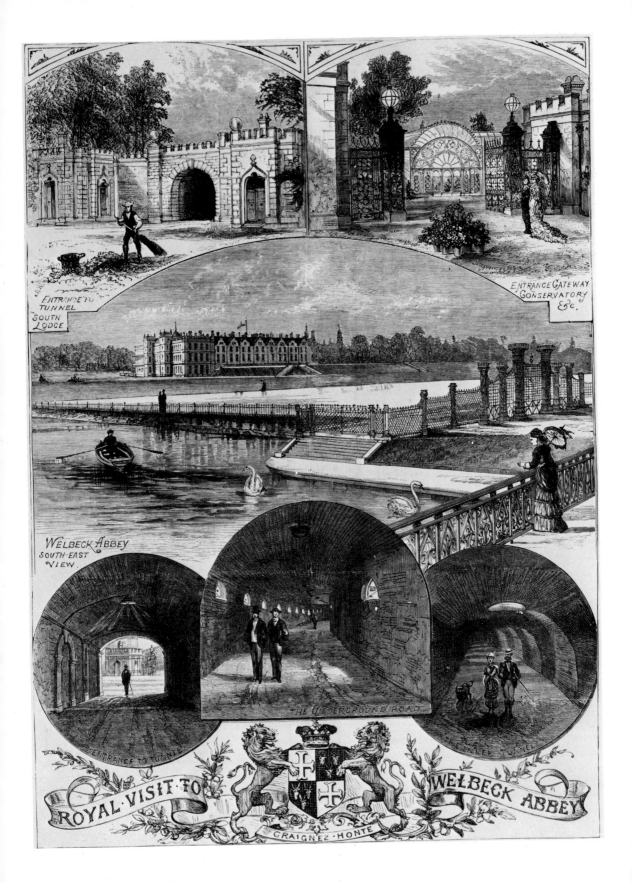

ENTRANCE TO
TUNNEL
SOUTH
LODGE

ENTRANCE GATEWAY
CONSERVATORY
&c.

WELBECK ABBEY
SOUTH-EAST
VIEW.

THE UNDERGROUND ROAD

ENTRANCE TO TUNNEL

ROYAL VISIT TO

WELBECK ABBEY

CRAIGNEZ HONTE

the Crimean War, became increasingly peculiar in her habits after his death; she often astonished her guests by appearing at the dinner table as a Spanish dancer or a nun. In her final years she had her coffin placed in the hall and made her butler, Knighton, lift her into it at regular intervals, to make sure that it would be comfortable.[1]

Some of the landed aristocrats developed an excessive passion for privacy, a fairly common characteristic among those whose wealth is so great that it undermines human relationships with suspicion. Henry Cavendish, the millionaire scientist who died in 1810, lived the life of a recluse, communicating with his housekeeper mainly through scribbled notes left on a hall table; he refused to see any other female servant and ordered her immediate dismissal if he did. A similar rule was enforced at Woburn Abbey by the tenth Duke of Bedford who died in 1893: any woman servant who crossed his path after noon, by which time her work was supposed to be finished, was liable to be dismissed. The first Lord Astor, who was born in New York but became a British citizen, was also something of a recluse. He was so greatly terrified of assassination that he slept alone, with only his male secretary for company, in Hever Castle, where even guests were not admitted at night, being confined to the house which he had built specially for them in the grounds.

Eccentric misanthropy was carried to its ultimate degree by the fifth Duke of Portland, a descendant of Hans Bentinck, a Dutchman who was ennobled after he had helped to arrange the marriage between William III of Orange and Mary, daughter of James II. His great passion in life was digging underground rooms and tunnels and the grounds of Welbeck Abbey were honeycombed with his work. His masterpiece was one tunnel, a mile and a quarter long, which was wide enough to admit the passage of two carriages. It was lit by gas where it dipped below the lake. Lady Ottoline Morrell, who became a notable literary hostess in the period between the two world wars, recalls how, as a little girl, she made her first visit to Welbeck Abbey with her half-brother after he had inherited the title in 1879. 'The front drive was a grass-grown morass covered with builder's rubbish and to enable the carriage to reach the front door they had to put down temporary planks. The hall inside was without a floor. . . .

'His love of building tunnels came perhaps from an exaggerated desire for privacy. . . . When he travelled he never left his own carriage, but had it placed on a railway truck on the train and kept the green silk blind tightly drawn. . . .

'In the great kitchen the Duke's perpetual chicken was always roasting on a spit, so that whenever he should ring for it one should be ready roasted and in a fit state for eating. From this kitchen the food was lowered by a lift into a heated truck, which ran on rails through one of the underground passages into the house, a distance of about 150 yards.'[2]

In spite of the size of Welbeck Abbey, the duke lived in only four or five barely-furnished rooms, with brass letter boxes for

Welbeck Abbey, above and below ground at the time of a royal visit in 1881.

incoming and outgoing correspondence. All the other rooms were painted pink, and were completely bare except for lavatories in a corner.

The great wealth of the landed aristocrats allowed them to indulge their individual passion, whether it was for tunnelling, politics, shooting, or the collecting of erotic literature, like the Liberal prime minister, the fifth Earl of Rosebery and the first Lord Houghton, who assembled what was probably the biggest private collection of *erotica* of all times.[3] Eccentricity was not total, but it was common enough to make a deep impression on one young American, Henry Brooks Adam, the grandson of the sixth President of the United States, who accompanied his father to England when he became U.S. Minister in 1861. In his autobiography, published much later, he wrote: 'Eccentricity was so general as to become hereditary distinction. It made the chief charm of England society as well as its chief terror.'[4] This self-gratification helped to dissipate the energies of the hereditary leaders of society who still commanded an inordinate share of the national wealth; but there were gradations of rank within the aristocracy, and, lower down, most of them chose to live a more conventional life, which was, however, rarely untouched by magnificence, and ostentatious splendour. Many visiting and resident Americans succumbed to the 'charm' and ignored the 'terror'. Nathaniel Parker Willis, who made a living by writing poetry which is no longer read and by soliciting invitations from the English and Scottish aristocracy, was one of the first Americans in Victorian times to be captivated by the pleasures of the English country house. 'An arrival in a strange house in England', he wrote, 'seems to a foreigner almost magical. The absence of all bustle consequent on the same event abroad—the silence, respectfulness, and self-possession of the servants—the ease and expedition with which he is installed in a luxurious room, almost with his second breath under the roof— his portmanteau unstrapped, his toilet laid out, his dress shoes and stockings at his feet, and the fire burning as if he had sat by it the whole day—it is like the golden facility of a dream.'[5] Although Mrs Harriet Beecher Stowe seems to have had some initial reservations about servants and their masters and mistresses, these soon evaporated in the warm charm of her reception so that she became one of the main apologists for the Duke of Sutherland's brutal clearance of his crofters from his vast estates in the Highlands. While Henry James, who became obsessed by the theme of the confrontation of innocence and experience, of the contrasting American and English civilis-ations, wrote in 1879: 'Of all the great things that the English have invented and made a part of the credit of the national character, the most perfect, the most characteristic, the one they have mastered most completely in all its details, so that it has become a compendious illustration of their social genius and their manners, is the well-appointed, well-administered, well-filled country house.'[6]

Wollaton Hall, which remained the family seat of the Willoughbys of Middleton until it was sold to Nottingham Corporation in 1925, was but a single representative example of the many great houses which could be found in all the shires and counties of England in Victorian times. Surrounded by a vast deer park, where 1,200 fallow deer and a smaller number of the noble red deer ran wild, the sixteenth-century house, with its 365 windows, one for each day of the year, was approached by a drive, bordered by ninety-foot-high lime trees, which was three-quarters of a mile long. Statues of subjects from Roman mythology were scattered in the grounds, discreetly hidden

Wollaton Hall, Nottinghamshire, the south front.

behind trees, where they had been placed on the orders of a former Lady Middleton so that their embarrassing nudity should not be visible from the terrace. The house had *two* wine cellars, one forty-two feet by twenty feet, and another smaller cellar, which was only thirty-six feet by twelve, stocked with the choicest port, sherry, Madeira and table wines and containing also a huge vat, resting on wooden trestles, which could hold 1,500 gallons of ale. Although the vat was no longer used, one seventy-year-old servant, who had entered service at the hall at the age of six, could still remember the times when it had been full.

At the back of the house, approached through a noble arched gateway, flanked by ornamental pillars, stood the stables, with separate stalls capable of accommodating up to sixty horses. A piece of oak, which had been used as a mounting block by a former Lord Middleton some thirty-five years before, was still preserved and in the course of time it had become as hard and as black as ebony. The coach house contained six or seven dark-blue carriages, drags, omnibuses and the old family coach, whose panels were emblazoned with heraldic bearings and the family motto, 'Truth without Fear'. The bakery, the laundry, a separate fowl-plucking house and some of the servants' bedrooms were situated nearby. A walled kitchen garden of nine acres contained 9,700 square feet of glass and forcing houses for peaches, grapes, melons and cucumbers to supply the Middleton's dining table.[7]

These country houses were far more than a home: they were a bizarre combination of a luxury hotel, a business headquarters, a museum, a wine merchant's warehouse, and an art gallery, while their grounds were a combination of a noble pleasure park and a model farm. The cost of maintaining such establishments was immense, particularly as many of the landed aristocrats owned more than one country house and additionally, a large Georgian town house in a gracious London square, which was their equivalent of the modern *pied-à-terre*. Even quite early in the reign, some aristocrats were already beginning to feel the strain: as Emerson said, 'their many houses eat them up.'[8] Apart from any questions of status, they were forced to employ a staff of servants which was sufficiently large to minister to all the real and simulated needs of their own family and their guests, and also to look after the other unoccupied homes on a care and maintenance basis. When the family left their London residence, taking most of the servants and the valuable gold and silver plate with them, the remaining staff rolled up the carpets; stacked the chairs by the walls; enveloped the larger items of furniture in dust covers and the curtains in hessian sacking; placed sheets of brown paper over the pictures; protected the door handles and the lamps with brown paper or hessian; and then settled down to celebrate the weeks of profitable independence ahead on board-wages, which were given to them in lieu of food.

Although servant accommodation was often spartan even in the most magnificent houses, an excessive consciousness of rank, which was no less pronounced downstairs than it was upstairs, made it necessary to provide many extra bedrooms and workrooms for the servant hierarchy. One Victorian architect recommended that the house steward, who was the senior servant, should be provided with a small suite of rooms, consisting of an office, a sitting room big enough to be used as a dining room for all the upper servants, and a bedroom with a safe or a strongroom for his papers. The butler should have a pantry with a specially constructed repository for the valuable plate and a separate scullery if the plate was frequently in use. In addition he might also have an adjoining bedroom. The housekeeper, the senior female servant, would need a parlour which was sufficiently roomy to store all her home-made preserves, cakes, biscuits and pickles, plus some of the china and the glass. The parlour would have to be big enough to entertain upper servants at some meals. Adjoining, there should be a stillroom, equipped with a small range, a covered lead sink, and a confectioner's oven, where the cakes and biscuits could be made. Nearby, it

The thirty-three domestic servants of Hanham Hall, Suffolk, 1883.

would be convenient to have a cool, well-ventilated storeroom for groceries and possibly a separate china closet with its own attached scullery. Then there were the ladies' maids. They would need their own separate sitting room, where they could also do their sewing and their clear starching at a side table. In addition, the first-rate establishment might also provide a separate brushing room, a knife room, a shoe room and a lamp room.

The lower servants would eat in the servants' hall, which could be barely furnished with a long central table, a sufficient number of chairs, pinrails for hats and cloaks, a jack towel roller, and possibly some lockers. It was suggested, for fairly obvious reasons, that the men's sleeping quarters should be some distance away from those of the maids. The men could be accommodated in separate rooms or in a partitioned dormitory; while the maids could sleep, two to a room, in the attics. The upper servants, that is the house steward, the butler, the male cook, the ladies' maids, the valet, would need their own bedrooms. Equivalent sleeping accommodation would, of course, have to be provided for upper servants who accompanied their masters and mistresses on visits to the house.[9]

Conspicuous display, a sensitivity to status both upstairs and

Charity begins at home. At Cusworth Hall, Yorkshire, the mistress and her staff prepare to serve tea to troops stationed in the area just before the outbreak of the First World War.

downstairs, and the consequent waste of time, money and resources all added to the expenditure of the landed aristocrat. At the beginning of Queen Victoria's reign the estimated household expenses of the fourth Earl of Ashburnham were £2,742 a year, say thirteen to eighteen times the salary of a country curate or one hundred and twenty times the wages of a farm labourer. Of the total, £769 went on wages and house labour, £200 on servants' beer and another £138 on liveries and hats, about 40 per cent in all.[10] Despite the agricultural depression which breathed coldly on the fortunes of many landed proprietors in the 1870s and the even more icy blast of estate duties some twenty years later, many of them continued to retain their fortunes—and their large staffs of servants—to the end of the reign. The Duke of Westminster, who was one of the richest men in England, and the sixth Duke of Portland, each employed about three hundred servants, about the same number as the Queen herself, who had a separate staff of Indian cooks just to prepare a curry lunch each day whether anyone wanted to eat it or not. Some of the incredible waste in the royal kitchens is recalled by Gabriel Tschumi, who became an apprentice at Buckingham Palace in 1898. Dozens of pheasants, salmon, sturgeon, trout, *foie gras*, soufflés made with four or five dozen eggs all found their way from time to time into the rubbish bins in the cause of gastronomic perfection. A year before he started working there, twenty-four extra cooks had been brought from France to prepare the fourteen-course banquet in celebration of the queen's diamond jubilee; the main course *rosettes de saumon au rubis* (cold salmon in claret jelly) had to be made three times before it received the approval of the Royal chef.[11]

Only the wealthiest and the most spendthrift could afford to live on such a scale and the more representative Duke of Richmond and Gordon had to be content with a modest staff of thirty-eight men and women, including ten housemaids, some of whom were, surprisingly, paid by cheque.[12] Forty or fifty servants remained about the norm for those great landowners who were able to hold their head above water in the turbulent Victorian age. What distinguished the noblest households from the majority in the land was the conspicuous number of male indoor servants—one of the main indicators of precedence and rank in Victorian times. At the beginning of the reign a French cook (the ultimate status symbol) could demand £150 or £200 or more a year; a house steward might get £75, which was almost double what an experienced housekeeper might expect to receive. At the bottom of the servant hierarchy, the under housemaid or the scullion might have been paid £9 or £10 a year in noble households, and even less elsewhere.

To employ men instead of women servants created many additional expenses. A tax on male servants had been introduced by Lord North in 1777 to help pay for the cost of fighting the Americans and by 1808, when Britain was involved in an even more prolonged war against the French, it had reached the fantastic figure for those days of just over £7 a year for each male servant if there were eleven or more in the household. Although it was progressively reduced, until it had reached 15 shillings a year in 1869, a figure which remained unaltered until the tax was rather tardily abolished in 1937, this tax and other imposts on conspicuous display created a considerable financial burden. In 1843 the Earl of Ashburnham, for example, paid taxes for the half-year of £21 15s 9d for his male servants, another £11 for his four-wheeled carriages, and £1 4s for armorial bearings, plus a ten per cent surcharge.[13] The cost of keeping powdered footmen was also increased by a duty on hair powder, which lasted from 1786 to 1869, though some employers forced their footmen to economise by using ordinary household flour on their hair instead, while other footmen cheated their employers by using

flour but continuing to claim their annual allowance of £1 or £2 for powder.

In addition, footmen and other male servants in livery had to be provided with specially tailored suits. In the 1850s a footman's suit of the best quality cost three guineas at Doudneys of Old Bond Street and Burlington Arcade. In most households footmen were allowed two new suits a year; their old liveries usually ended up on stalls at Houndsditch Old Clothes Exchange in London, where they were eagerly sought by exporters, who usually shipped them off to German fairs to be sold 'for the purpose of making facings for some of the civic officials of the Northern powers'.[14]

Examples of specially tailored livery for male staff in 1881. From left to right, footman, coachman, and a coachman wearing his box coat.

The great age of the male servant had passed by the time Queen Victoria came to the throne. Some had only just disappeared, like the running footman in his cutaway coat and silk, knee-length petticoat-breeches, weighted down by a heavy gold or silver fringe, who would run at a steady 7 mph in front of his master's coach, pausing only occasionally for a sip of white wine mixed with egg which he carried in a silver, ball-shaped container at the top of his long staff. (One applicant for this post with the fourth Duke of Queensberry, who was being publicly tested for his pace in Piccadilly, used his turn of speed for personal profit by running off in the Duke's livery, which was never seen again, though it probably ended up on a stall at Houndsditch.) The sewer, who waited personally at table upon lords and kings, had vanished many centuries before, and even the male cook was becoming a rarity. Higher wages, taxes, and additional expenses all combined to reduce the number of male servants even more in Victorian times. Although the figures are not strictly comparable, because of changes in methods of classification, the official census of England and Wales shows that the total number was reduced from 74,323 in 1851 to 58,527 in 1891.[15] Only the wealthiest could afford to employ the full range of house steward, groom of the chambers, valet, cook, butler, under-butler, footmen, usher, page and 'tiger', plus coachmen, grooms and gardeners. Others, whose income at the beginning of the reign amounted to no more than £1,000 or £1,200 a year were advised to be content with a single male servant or, if they had only £600 or £700, with a footboy.[16]

Employment as a footboy to a clergyman, a lady, or a farmer, whose fortune did not match their social aspirations, was one of the methods by which a lad could enter service in the first half of the nineteenth century, though it was more common, and usually more satisfactory, to obtain some less ostentatious position on a large estate instead. 'Footboy' was often a euphemism for 'general dogsbody' or 'man-of-all-work', as Henry White found in 1837 when, at the age of fifteen, he started to work for Dr Sisson, the rector of Duntisborne, Gloucestershire. In addition to his more formal duties in livery, he was expected to clean the boots and the knives, to do some gardening, to act as 'groom and coachman' for the rector's only conveyance—a humble donkey cart—and, in his spare time, to make himself generally useful! His livery, which had been tailored for him in the neighbouring town of Cirencester, would not have disgraced the footman of a lord. It consisted of a conventional full dress suit of 'low shining shoes, white stockings, black plush breeches, with bright buckle and buttons at the knees, a brilliant brimstone-coloured waistcoat, covered by a bright sky-blue coat, pigeon-tailed, of course, with stand-up collar, embroidered with two rows of gold braid, and finishing with a set of yellow buttons.' When he tried it on, he was then summoned to the drawing room, where his 'young mistress was pleased to make some

'Horray, Hooray! 'Ere's a Johnny with his calf falled down.' A Victorian footman experiencing difficulty with his 'falsies'.

allusion to the smallness of my legs, but this, as the Doctor sagely remarked, was an evil which would grow less every day.'

An even worse ordeal followed on the Sunday when he had to undertake the normal duties of a footman by following the family to church, opening their pew door, and placing their prayer books on the seat. The news of his first public appearance in what he disparagingly called his 'magpie livery' had circulated rapidly, and he had to endure the boisterous banter of the village boys and girls who had assembled to watch his début. Late in life he could still remember how his blood had reached 'boiling point'.[17]

Such an event, which must have been humiliating for a sensitive boy, could not have happened to a footman in a household of the first rank, where the villagers, whatever was happening in their minds and hearts, would have been so preoccupied in bowing and curtseying to the local lord that they would have had no time to jeer at his footman. But the footman, as the most public and the most outrageous symbol of divisions in society, was often made the butt of working-class ridicule when he was out alone; street urchins delighted to defile his white

Flamboyant, full-dress liveries of footman, coachman and pages in 1911.

stockings with handfuls of mud and even, if they had the chance, to prick his calves with a pin to see if he was wearing 'falsies', which could be painful if his legs had natural curves. American tourists were alternately shocked and amused at the sight of footmen. Catherine Sedgwick from Massachusetts, thought that there must be something 'rotten in the state' when men 'look up to a station behind a lord's coach as a privileged place', but ended by laughing at 'their fantastical liveries.'[18]

Footmen, however, became accustomed to disparagement, including some from upper servants in the house, and soon acquired their own patina of supercilious protection, and many of them delighted to parade their flamboyance in the streets. Outdoors, with their full dress livery, they wore white gloves and a cocked hat, which was replaced later in the century by a top hat with a colourful cockade. In noble households, they also had an indoor livery with a dress coat instead of a tail coat and pumps instead of buckled shoes and sometimes also a less formal dress, consisting in the later part of the century of white tie and tails with brass livery buttons stamped with their lord's crest. However pleased they might have been with their own

appearance, there was one necessity which brought little delight to any footman. The daily powdering of the hair was an undignified and unpleasant process, involving the use of plenty of soap and water to work up a stiff lather, which was then carefully combed so that the tooth marks showed in even rows, before the powder or ordinary flour was applied. Late at night, when duties were done, the hair had to be washed and oiled to free it from the clogging detritus.

Footmen were chosen for their good looks and their height: most of them were over six feet tall and extra inches could add a few pounds each year to their pay. ('All the little fellows', James Fenimore Cooper noticed, 'sink into pot-boys, grooms, stable men, and attendants at the inns.'[19]) In the best households, footmen were matched in height to avoid any risible incongruity in their joint appearance, and they were trained to act in unison, marching in stately step up to the great doors of a London house and banging on the double knockers in perfect harmony, before they marched back again to their lady waiting in her coach. Their prospects in service were usually blighted if they did not

Punch turns an ironic eye on the indolence of mid-Victorian aristocrats, male and female. The caption read, 'Why they don't marry.'

grow tall enough: one 24-year-old Scotsman, who in his own words was not 'a six-foot man, nor yet particularly handsome', wrote despairingly to a magazine in 1849 to inquire whether he would find better fortune as a servant or a waiter in America or Australia.[20]

The grandest establishments normally had three footmen, whose duties varied according to the customs of the household. The first footman, often known as 'James', whatever his own Christian name might be, usually acted as the lady's footman. Among his other duties, he had to prepare both her early-morning and breakfast trays; to take her dog for a walk; to clean

'Not meeting his match. The new footman.' A mistress casts a disparaging glance at an undersized applicant for the post of footman. It was essential that footmen should be neatly matched in height.'

her shoes; to brush the mud off her riding habit and the hems of her long dresses; and in some houses to scrub the small silver coins to ensure that they were uninfected by any previous handling of tradesmen. Sometimes, he himself was responsible for paying small charges for toll gates, cabs and postage stamps, expenses which he would later reclaim from the house steward. The expenses of one illiterate first footman in 1858 included 'cab to station', 2s; 'Whaterlow Bridge' which was quite a bargain for 2d; and '4 days bord wages', 8s.[21] The second footman helped to lay the luncheon table; sometimes acted as valet to the eldest son; and often had to clean all the mirrors in the house. The third footman carried coals and wood and did other similar tasks and deputised for the others as he gained experience. Both the first and second footman had to wait at table, and the first footman often accompanied his lady when she went to dine at another house, his main duty being to stand behind her chair to increase the impression of her great rank and status. Footmen had to answer the front door in the afternoon; go out with the carriage at any time of the day or night; and usually also cleaned the plate, though this work was sometimes shared with an under-butler.

Cleaning the valuable gold or silver plate was one of the footman's most important and tiresome duties. One former servant recommended that each article should be cleaned separately so that none would be scratched. The plate should be sponged clean of grease before the moistened plate powder was rubbed in with the hand. The longer it was rubbed, the greater would be the shine. When the plate was clean, all the powder should be brushed out of the crevices of crests and ornamental work and the gaps between the prongs of forks, before it was finished with a leather.[22] Many servants had their own special tips for cleaning plate. If it was tarnished, said one, use spirits of wine; if scratched, use rotten stone and oil on a woollen stocking, never silk, said another.

When a footman had served his lengthy apprenticeship, he might aspire to join the upper servants by applying for a post as a valet or a butler, though until the 1890s he could scarcely have hoped to obtain the latter position until he was thirty years of age at least. The valet, or 'gentleman's gentleman', who was sometimes though by no means invariably foreign, acquired a superficial gentility through close association with his master in sporting events, social engagements and travel (though the valet travelled in a second class railway coach while his master used the first): and his acquaintance with the latest gossip in society made him a figure of some authority in the steward's room where it was his privilege to dine with other upper servants. He was inclined to wear rings and to have his hair cut in a fashionable style and, as he did not have to wear livery, he could dress like a man-about-town, though never in such a flamboyant way that

Female servants pamper a London footman exhausted at the end of a season.

he outshone his master, whose discarded clothes were one of the valet's perquisites. His main task, like that of the lady's maid in relation to her mistress, was to ensure that his gentleman appeared to best advantage in the world, well-dressed, well-served and immaculate, with his mind so freed from the encumbrances of mundane life that he was able to devote his whole attention to the chit-chat of society.

Half an hour before his master rose, the valet would collect his clean shoes, his brushed clothes, his pot of tea and bread and butter from the stillroom, his hot water for shaving, his letters and his newspaper and take them to the gentleman's bedroom. After he had opened the shutters and drawn the curtains, he would empty the wash basin into a slop pail, clean the basin with a cloth, put the shaving can in the basin, not forgetting to cover the can with a cloth to keep the water hot. After the valet had inquired what his master wished to wear that day, he would place the required suit neatly on the seat of a chair, with socks and underclothes on top, and then put the studs and cuff-links in an appropriate shirt before he placed it over the back of the chair. After he had prepared the bath, he would take away his master's evening clothes (which were, of course, worn every night) so that he could brush and press them downstairs.

Most gentlemen did not require full assistance in dressing, but if his master was elderly or otherwise incapacitated, say through a fall on the hunting field or through imbibing an inordinate quantity of alcohol on the previous night, the bell would ring, and the valet would dash upstairs from his half-finished breakfast to find his gentleman bathed and waiting in his underclothes for his valet's personal attentions. 'You throw the dress shirt over his head', wrote one servant who had dressed many a gentleman in his time, 'and fasten the front studs, hand the trousers and fasten braces, put on collar and tie the tie, assist on with waistcoat, jacket or coat, and put on socks and shoes.'[23] The valet also had sometimes to comb and to part his master's hair.

After these preliminaries, both were almost ready for the social fray. The valet was expected to have a good knowledge of Bradshaw; some acquaintance with foreign languages, although this was often rudimentary; an expert knowledge of flies, rods and lines; and to be quick in loading guns. (He would have needed to be extra swift with Earl de Grey, later the Marquis of Ripon, who was reputed, between 1867 and 1900, to have slaughtered no less than 370,000 animals and birds, including two rhinoceros, eleven tigers, twelve buffalo, ninety-seven pigs, 186 deer, 27,686 hare, 56,460 grouse, 97,759 partridge and 142,343 pheasant.)[24]

Although the valet's duties may seem quite simple to the uninitiated, he needed a vast amount of equipment if he was to do his work well. One former valet recommended that he should have trees for top boots and walking shoes; shoe brushes, black and brown; clothes-brushes, narrow hat and button; a button stick; sand or emery paper; a boot bone; chamois leathers, dusters and cleaning rags; breeches paste and breeches ball; brush for red hunting coat and sponges; American cloth; painter's white overall, apron and chemicals; hat iron; dubbin; grease brush; old tooth brush; oil for fishing lines; gun oil, cartridge bags, boot top tags and spare boot and shoe laces.[25] In other words, he had to be prepared. The valet was far more immediately and continuously exposed to the whims, peccadilloes and temperament of his employer; but, in compensation, he had a more varied and outgoing life.

The butler also needed all the skills and knowledge of the valet, particularly as retrenchment in late Victorian times often resulted in the two posts being combined except in the richest households; but his main duties lay elsewhere. He was personally responsible for the conduct of the footmen; the custody of the plate; and the control of the cellar. It was this final function which helped to give him his not always undeserved alcoholic reputation, for in the earlier years of the reign at least, table wine, apart from champagne, was still delivered to a nobleman's cellar in casks and, as 'A Practical Man' advised, it was incumbent on the butler that the contents 'should be often tasted, to be assured of their state, that any deterioration may be prevented in time'.[26] The butler was also responsible for the brewing of the servants' beer, the arrangement of the dining table, the announcement of dinner and the carving of joints in fashionable homes where dinner was served *à la Russe* from side tables.

Jeeves-like, through the gradual disappearance of other more highly-paid male servants, the butler has come down to modern times as *the* archetypal manservant, benign to his employers, haughty with inferiors, privy to all the family gossip, and a bulwark of sound advice and sensible conduct in any crisis; but in Victorian times his status was more lowly. Above him, both in rank and pay, there were the valet, the groom of the chambers and the house steward. The groom of the chambers was a sort of super-butler, tall, suave, and even more distinguished in appearance, who somehow contrived to appear, miraculously, whenever there was a door to be opened, a window blind to be lowered or raised, an inkpot to be filled, or a new sheaf of hand-made, crested notepaper to be placed on the writing tables. His last duty at night, before the introduction of electric lighting, was to give each lady and gentleman a candlestick as they went up to bed. At the apex of the servant hierarchy was the house steward, who was finally responsible for the smooth functioning of the household and the transition from one house to another at the beginning and the end of the season or at any other time. He engaged and dismissed lower servants and controlled the main household accounts. Sometimes, when very important guests were present, he might condescend to wait at table.

Even in the richest households the male servants were usually outnumbered by female servants by about three to one. There were ladies' maids, cooks, housemaids, laundry maids, kitchen

The housekeeper.

maids, scullions and, when there were children in the house, nursemaids and governesses; but as most of these were more frequently found in upper middle-class homes, too, where their work and their functions were not dissimilar, consideration of them may be left until a later chapter. But it would be impossible to leave the nobleman's house without mentioning the housekeeper, who often became a legend in her own lifetime and occasionally stayed on in spirit form to haunt the ancestral home over which she had ruled. 'Housekeeper' like 'painter' is an ambiguous term. There was no connection between the housekeeper who performed all the functions of a housewife (including sometimes concubinage) in the modest home of a tradesman, a clerk, or a hairdresser, and the woman who was the chief female servant in an ancestral home.

The rich man's housekeeper, dressed formidably in black with an immaculate white frilled cap of lace and ribbons and a chatelaine at her waist or a huge bunch of keys in her hand, was a figure of awe to lower servants. Under housemaids sometimes trembled (literally) at her approach and feared her more than they did their mistress. 'This middle-aged woman', wrote one reviewer in 1854, 'knows their ways—and is ever on the watch. Her vigilance and her tyranny are not to be matched in any drawing room.'[27] Even young manservants often shared the maids' terror. Albert Thomas, who was third footman to the Duke of Norfolk in 1900, recalls how he went to bathe the feet of the eighteen-stone butler who was suffering from gout. On his return to the servants' hall, he told the other servants that it was lucky the crabbed old winepusher wasn't a centipede, for every foot he had was gouty. His remark raised a laugh, but the

Harriet Rogers, cook-housekeeper at Erddig photographed in 1911, her fifty-eighth year of service.

merriment was short-lived, as the words had been heard by the housekeeper. 'That was awful,' Thomas wrote. 'I had rather his grace had heard us, he was human, but her—Oh, 'Lor, we did cop it.'[28] As a mark of respect, the housekeeper was always addressed as 'Mrs', regardless of her marital state.

She had few formal duties, though in the best houses it was her custom to receive the mistress or the master after their return from any visit, or even from a longish drive, by standing at the top of the main stairs, which she also did when week-end guests arrived so that she could show them to their rooms. Her main domain was the storeroom, the linen cupboard, the china closet and the stillroom, to which she held the keys, and woe betide the poor maid who broke a cup or failed to mend some linen neatly. The ghosts of these tyrannical women lived on to strike terror into the hearts of future generations. One Victorian author, who made a special study of hauntings in ancestral homes, found that they usually involved housekeepers, seldom butlers and never footmen. One of the most celebrated ghosts was that of Helen Bell, a housekeeper who was murdered by two thieves at a mansion near Edinburgh in the eighteenth century; he claimed to have found other housekeeper-hauntings, but the owners of the houses were often reluctant to admit to them publicly for fear of terrifying their guests.[29]

Status Below Stairs

Even when all allowance has been made for deference, Victorian servants seem to have had a genuine respect for aristocratic masters and mistresses. In one of the earliest pieces of investigative journalism by a group of women writers, the crusading *British Weekly* sent a team of what it called 'commissioners' into contrasting districts of London in 1889 to discover how servants were really treated in different situations, ranging from elegant society homes to Jewish houses in East End ghettos. Through her contact with the manager of a fashionable West End grocers, one commissioner was invited to meet twenty assorted servants in his suburban home. At the meeting, one valet described how he had entered the house by the front door on his first day in a new situation, only to be greeted by his master, who had conducted him outside, shown him the area gate, and told him always to use that entrance. The valet went on: 'It's only the aristocracy who treat servants properly. I tried one situation out of aristocratic circles, and that was where the man showed me his·area gate. The aristocracy know how to behave to a gentleman, even if he happens to be a servant.' Another servant said: 'It's only in second-class houses that they treat servants without any consideration. But it isn't everyone can get into a big house.'[1]

Just as there were second-class houses so were there second-class servants; rank and precedence were as divisive downstairs as they were upstairs. Lower servants rarely benefited from any intimacy of contact with either upper servants or their employers. In some of the best houses, the maids were so remote from their employers that they rarely saw them, owing to the custom, which was hardened into an adamantine rule in some households, that maids should be doubly penalised in comparison with the children of the house, by being neither seen nor heard, except at the daily family prayers. In one great house, at least, the maids had to face the wall if they happened to meet their master or their mistress in the corridor.

The sense of status was no less strong downstairs, being symbolised by what the lower servants irreverently called the 'pugs' procession'. In most big houses all the servants would eat the first course of their dinner together in the servants' hall, sometimes in enforced silence; but when that course was finished, the upper servants would rise and file out of the hall in order of precedence, in some houses carrying their plate of pudding, and in others going empty-handed to the steward's or the house-keeper's room where it would be served. These distinctions were extended to the normal world outside: butlers and other upper servants from neighbouring houses had their own public house, or club as they called it, which they patronised, while footmen met together in another club.

Reflected rank illuminated the dim confines of life downstairs. According to Lady Augusta Fane it was usual for valets and ladies' maids to address each other by the names of their

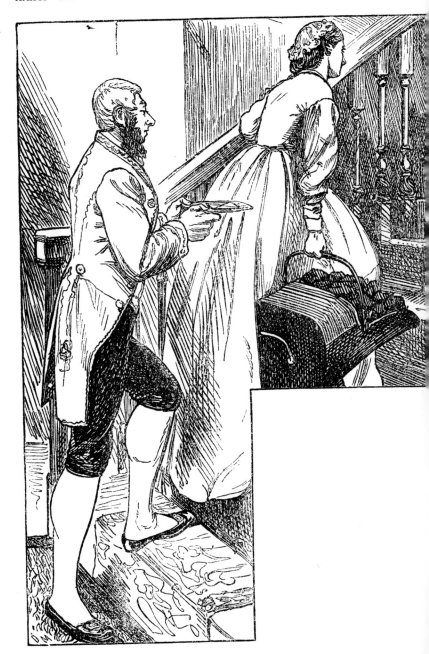

There was no chivalry below stairs in Victorian England. The maid carries the coals while the footman struggles up with a single letter.

aristocratic employers, so that a valet might call out to a lady's maid, 'Hurry up, Ripon, you'll be late for supper, both the Abercorns are down.' These personal servants' intimate acquaintance with the niceties of social life made them far more conscious of distinctions. One lady's maid told her untitled employer that she wanted to leave her service because 'it hurts my feelings always to have to walk last from the Hall. I want to take a situation with a titled lady, or at least an honourable.'[2]

Not surprisingly, perhaps, many visitors from the United States were particularly perplexed by the downstairs reverence for rank, this 'relic of barbarism', as Adam Badeau, consul-

Punch delighted in making fun of servants' aspirations or 'servantgalism'. In this cartoon a refined maid is resigning because 'the hother servants is so 'orrid vulgar, and hignorant.'

general in London in the 1870s, called it, a feature of social life which he found so greatly incongruous 'in the country of Carlyle and Bright, of Huxley and Mill'. He found many examples of this strange form of downstairs snobbery and gave as one instance that of a woman cook who took a situation with a baronet, but left immediately when she found that he was also actually working as a doctor.[3] Americans were even more puzzled by downstairs distinctions. One 'American Lady', writing home from London in 1843, was surprised to find such 'an aristocracy in servitude' that 'the housemaid may not use a veil or a parasol' but both were permitted to a lady's maid.[4]

Mrs Bancroft, the wife of the United States Minister to England from 1846 to 1849, soon discovered that her own lady's maid would not take tea with a housemaid or a footman. 'The division of labour,' she wrote, 'or rather ceremonies, between the butler and the footman I have now mastered, I believe in some degree, but that between the *upper* and the *under* housemaid is still a profound mystery to me, though the upper has explained to me for the twentieth time that she did only "the top of the work".'[5] The upper housemaid was mainly responsible for the appearance of the room, the curtains, chair covers, ornaments, plants and flowers; while the under housemaid did the hard

'Fashions for the kitchen.'
Cook: 'Lor', Jane, I wouldn't be bothered with them "Trains" every day! I only wears mine on Sundays!'
Jane: 'That may do for *you* Cook; but for my part I likes to be a lady weekdays as well as Sundays!'

physical work of sweeping, polishing, cleaning grates and laying fires.

Demarcation disputes were so common downstairs that, in comparison, a modern manufacturing plant appears to be a haven of industrial peace. A footman refused to hand his mistress's clean shoes to the lady's maid, and she refused to pick them up from the corridor where he had placed them.[6] Most ladies' maids, who were second only to housekeepers in status, balked at mending gentlemen's underclothes, forcing valets to find a friendly housemaid who might do the work as a favour. A young American had some personal experience of servants' demarcation disputes while he was making a tour of ancestral homes in the 1870s. When Richard Henry Dana, the son of his more famous father, was staying with Earl Spencer at Althorp, he was astonished to find that he and Lord Charles Bruce had to whitewash the lines on the grass court before they could have a game of tennis, even though 'there were standing about an abundance, both outdoors and in, of men quite capable of doing this work'. It was the man-of-all-work's job, but he could not be found, and 'neither the gardener, nor the footmen, nor the valets, nor the bootblacks nor, of course, the maids would help. Our hostess knew this so well that she did not even ask them.'[7]

'A Black Indignity'
Lady of the house: 'Oh, Thomas! Have the goodness to take up some coals into the nursery!'
Thomas: 'H'm, Ma'am! If you ask it a favour, Ma'am, I don't much object; but I 'ope you don't take me for an 'ousemaid, Ma'am.'

Servants were so jealous of their own domain that any intrusion could sometimes erupt into violence. Eric Horne was serving as a footman in a nobleman's house, when another footman 'put a kettle on the kitchen range to make the drawing room tea because no other fires were lit on that hot summer's day. The cook came at him with a long knife, shouting "Make your own fires" like a madman.'[8]

But it was not all fights, snobbery and woe downstairs in the big house. If you could accept, in the words of one Victorian footman that 'the life of a gentleman's servant is something like that of a bird shut up in a cage', there were considerable

compensations.[9] Like any other subject class, servants had learnt how to build an elaborate structure of defences. In theory, they were on display, or working, for many hours every day, but most of them, particularly the men, soon acquired a sixth sense which enabled them to anticipate the likely imposition of any unwelcome or extraneous task, from which they escaped by disappearing into some nether region of the house or by becoming engaged on an even more pressing duty. One Victorian man-servant, who saved enough in service to establish himself eventually as a bookseller in Hampstead, confessed that, 'Gentlemen's servants in some situations may have a deal of leisure upon their hands by a proper management of their business. I used to spend my leisure hours in reading and writing *as an amusement*.'[10] Few of the men strained themselves physically in the service of their employers, accepting, as one early feminist complained, 'only a light and lady-like share of anything that can be called housework.'[11]

Although accommodation was often poor, particularly for men, so that it was not unknown for second and third footmen to be allocated no more comfortable a sleeping place than the kitchen table, they usually found themselves some more comfortable berth and they did at least have a roof over their heads which was more than many people could boast in Victorian times. The cooking of the servants' meals was sometimes perfunctory or monotonous, but there were four ample meals a day—breakfast, dinner, tea, and supper—plus pickings from the upstairs plates for the enterprising or the hungry. Home-brewed beer was provided free, even at breakfast in some country houses. This was a legacy from the eighteenth century when imported tea was still too expensive to be drunk by any people but ladies and gentlemen. The normal allowance was one pint for men and half a pint for women at each meal; in some houses, beer money, usually 8d a day, was given instead. Wine was often provided free for upper servants and some of them acquired such a fine palate that it made them excessively discriminating in the employment they would take. One valet, who was being interviewed by a rich banker, politely inquired what varieties of wine were served at the steward's table and on being told that port and sherry were given, he remarked that he favoured Madeira himself.

'Why', said the banker, 'there is the Curate of the parish here cannot afford himself a glass of wine of any sort.'

'Ah', said the valet in reply. 'I always pitied that sort of gentleman.'[12]

Wages, which were usually paid quarterly in a nobleman's house, were very reasonable compared with those outside, as servants had virtually no other expenses but for clothes. In 1888 the house steward of the Duke of Richmond and Gordon received £100 a year; the groom of the chamber, £70; the valet, £60; and the butler, £45. The footmen received £26 to £34. There were two housekeepers, who were each paid £60 a year,

Male servants' expensive tastes in wine were often the subject of ironic mirth. The caption read:
Host: 'I don't like this Lafitte half so well as the last, Binns. Have you noticed any difference?'
New Butler: 'Well, sir, for myself I don't drink Claret; I find Port agrees with me so much better.'

41

the same wage as the cook. Ladies' maids received £26 to £28; the stillroom maid, £22; kitchen maids, £14 to £24; housemaids and laundry maids, £12 to £26; and the scullery maid, £12.[13] There were good chances of promotion and pensions were not unknown. The Duke had two retired men on the pay roll, who were sent £20 and £25 a year respectively by cheque. On those wages, even a lower servant could save, if he or she wished to do so, and many footmen had already accumulated £100 or more by their early twenties, which was enough to set up in some small business. Servants were great savers. The first savings bank was set up for servants in Bath by Lady Isabella Douglas in 1808. About a quarter to a half of all depositors in other early savings banks were servants: in York, 322 out of the first 670; in Lincoln, 49 out of the first hundred; and in Bolton, 44 out of the first two hundred.[14]

In addition to their regular wages, upper servants were traditionally entitled to a number of perquisites, and they also took others for themselves illicitly. Tradesmen were only too willing to give house stewards a cash discount on the bills so that they would continue to be favoured with the order. The cook, the housekeeper and the butler could also gain similar profits from the bills for their own departments. The cook also claimed the dripping from the roast meat as her right, while the groom of the chambers and the butler disputed the ownership of the ends of candles. Any butler who was worth his salt could gain one bottle of wine out of every six for himself. Although these minor peculations were a source of constant annoyance to employers, there was little they could do to stop them, unless they could detect some case of downright dishonesty in the accounts; but there was another practice to which most employers did openly object, the taking of vails or tips from guests, though even here their protests were often unavailing so that the practice continued in many houses far beyond Victorian times. The housemaid expected to find some silver coins or a half-sovereign under the pillow; the groom of the chambers wanted his sovereign for lighting the candles at night; the butler, not to be outdone, wanted a sovereign, too, for his personal favours and advice, and so did the footman if he had acted as valet to a guest who had arrived without one; while the gamekeeper expected to receive two guineas for a few days' shooting.

For this reason it could be quite expensive to stay as a guest at a country home, or even to make a conducted tour of one as many American visitors found to their cost. Nathaniel Hawthorne, who visited Byron's old home of Newstead Abbey in 1857, a popular attraction for American tourists, complained that he had to part with 'a good many shillings' to the housekeeper.[15] Calvin Colton, London correspondent of the New York *Observer* from 1831 to 1835, grumbled at 'the studied exactions' at Northumberland Castle.[16] The custom of demanding vails had been even more blatant in the previous century when servants actually lined up with outstretched hands to bid

The butler surprised. *Mistress*— 'James! I'm surprised . . .' *James*— 'So am I Mu'm! I thought you were out!'

farewell to departing guests.

Those guests who, in servant parlance, were 'mean' or 'not real gentlemen' were made to pay in other coin for their lack of generosity. The well-trained servant had been the victim of so many slights, indignities and affronts over the years that he had brought the art of studied insolence to perfection. A slightly raised eyebrow could alone express intense disapprobation. But he had a large repertoire of more obvious and annoying stratagems for expressing his disapproval of inconsiderate masters and mistresses or unwelcome guests: the banged door, the loud conversation, the dropped plate, the unanswered bell, the unreplenished fire and many more. Guests who had been 'mean' on their first visit usually suffered for it on the next. They would be met at the station in the dog cart instead of the more comfortable brougham; they would be ignored by the butler who was preoccupied with his effusive welcome for some more generous guest; they would be ill-placed at the shoot. One butler, Charles Cooper, had a great respect for most of the nobility with whom he had come into contact, but he did find 'one titled lady of a very old family who was most objectionable'. She had the annoying habit of delaying the serving of the dinner by refusing to tell the footmen immediately whether she wanted a particular course or not. The next time she came to dinner, Cooper had his revenge. 'I instructed the footman to place the hot dishes upon her hand if she still showed the same indifference and this had the desired effect.'[17].

Servants, who were often more conservative and conventional than their noble employers, expected all guests to conform to their own image of gentility. Richard Henry Dana must have looked anything but a gentleman when he arrived at Sir William Heathcote's home of Hursley Park, near Winchester, after a three-mile tramp from the station in pouring rain. He was wearing rough clothes, a cloth cap and his shoes were muddy. Even though he had a letter of introduction, the footman did not offer to take his cap and coat, but made him wait in the vestibule for what seemed to Dana to be half an hour.[18]

Sometimes even the most perfect servants could err in judgement. In 1895 when John James was working as a first footman to the Countess of Camperdown in London, there was a knock at the front door and he opened it onto an elderly man who was not very smartly dressed and was also clean-shaven, a suspicious sign in those days. Thinking that the visitor must be another servant, James directed him to a seat in the hall and asked him for his name, when the elderly man gave him his card. James looked at the card while he was walking up the stairs and 'nearly died of shock when I discovered that I had been condescending to His Grace the Duke of Westminster'. Then, in expiation not of his own snobbery but of his lack of perception, he adds: 'There are very few people who can afford to dress shabbily. . . . Indeed, it is very possible to be too much of a gentleman to be a gentleman at all.'[19]

'A delicate creature'
Mistress: (on her return from a visit) 'I don't understand, Smithers, this daily item of five shillings for dinners. I thought—'
Smithers: 'Well, Mu'm, the lower suvvants was so addicted to pork, Mu'm, I re'lly—I thought you wouldn't object to my having my meals helsewhere.'

'Manners'
Young mistress: 'Jane, I'm surprised that none of you stood up when I went into the kitchen just now!'
Jane: 'Indeed, Mu'm! We was much su'prised ourselves at your a comin' into the kitching while we was a 'avin' our luncheong!!'

Servants were constant and inflexible judges of others. Deep down in the servants' hall, the housekeeper's parlour, and the steward's room, every caller, every guest, every resident was tried daily *absente reo* before what Thackeray called 'the awful kitchen inquisition which sits in judgement in every house'. Behind the servants' mask of perfect politeness and consummate gentility, there were dark thoughts and hidden feelings, another world to which only the still innocent children of the house were ever admitted, where rumours echoed from the lofty ceilings and were magnified and distorted into malicious gossip and false report. The roots of the servant grapevine were embedded deep

Many employers believed, sometimes with justice, that their servants ate better than themselves. The caption read: 'Steak a little hard Ma'am? (Pause) We've a particular tender leg o'lamb in the hall—shall I inquire if you can have a slice of that, Ma'am?'

in the foundation of each great London house. A fragment of conversation overheard by a footman at the dinner table, or some actual confidence foolishly entrusted by some too in-genuous mistress to her maid, would be carried swiftly downstairs to the kitchen. From there it was transported lovingly up and down the neighbouring area steps by the visiting butterman and butcher to be deposited with that day's order on the great wooden tables in nearby kitchens, whence it could be disseminated to every part of the house by a word and a wink between the first and the second footman or by a whispered conversation between two under housemaids who shared the same room, and sometimes the same bed, in the cold and draughty attic.

Soon, each house in the square throbbed with the secret and

magnified report. Somewhere, a housekeeper would breathe it into the ear of her bored and idle mistress, who was possessed of sufficient malice to ignore the unwritten convention which prohibited her from listening to servants' gossip, so that, within the day, it would be dispensed with thin slices of bread and butter, macaroons and coffee biscuits to afternoon callers. The rumour would rage like some forest fire in society's drawing rooms and eventually it was bound to be swept back to the mistress of the house where it had originated, carried there by some previously slandered or slighted lady who hoped to gain her revenge by some oblique reference.

Tickled by a straw. A rare light moment in the lives of two young servants.

What a fury of accusations, recriminations, denials and protestations there would be between the mistress and her staff, but it was no more possible to trace the exact source of the rumour than it usually is to find the culprit for a forest fire. The damage had been done. A reputation had been besmirched. Servants could be dismissed, but the grapevine, with its myriad roots, went on and grew forever.

When rumour involved the servants' own prestige and authority, they could sometimes persuade their employers to become entangled in the most trivial disputes, as in the case of Eliza Mitchell, who was a scullery maid in the Earl of Ashburnham's household. Mrs Pilcher, who was the housekeeper to Sir Stratford Canning, was just about to poach Eliza and place her in her own kitchen, when the Earl's housekeeper heard of this foul, intended trespass. An acerb exchange of correspondence followed. On May 18, 1835, the Earl wrote to Sir Stratford:

> I am informed that a servant who is now in my service as Scullery maid is about to leave her situation in the hope of obtaining the place of kitchen maid in your Establishment. I should have deferred troubling you with any observations on this subject until you applied to me for the young woman's character, but as I am about to leave town tomorrow and the term of my absence is uncertain I will not defer until my return, the communication which I think it necessary to make to you.
>
> I will avow that circumstances make it inconvenient to me, to be deprived of the Scullery maid's services at the present moment—without the usual notice of a month's warning. But I deny that I should on this account above, say one word that might interfere with her prospects of better[ing] her situation. It has, however, come to my knowledge, that the girl who has never before been in London, but who has lived with her parents near my place in Sussex until she entered my service, and can therefore have few friends or advisers in town, has been prevailed upon by the inducements and promises held out by Mrs Pilcher.[20]

In spite of this initial stately salvo, victory in the battle over Eliza Mitchell went in the end to Mrs Pilcher, ably defended by her employer, Sir Stratford, who had gained some diplomatic skill through his long experience of negotiations over somewhat more momentous issues with the governments of Turkey, Greece, France and Russia.

In this case at least the interests of employers and their servants coincided, but they were to diverge increasingly as the reign progressed. The old family retainer had possessed such an intense loyalty that some of them were willing, literally, to brave cannon fire to ensure that their masters were well served. During the Battle of Sebastopol in the Crimean War, a civilian was observed walking between the Russian and the Allied lines, apparently oblivious of the bullets which were flying all around

The careful
Nurse

'Here's a treat, Missis's letters!!!'

'The Selfish' "please, m, I should
like my 'liday tomorrow, as my young man
has asked me to go to the 'lexander
pallis"'

50

The Studio Duster
"If I have rubbed it a bit, keep it off my weeks-money"

She was a very
light Sleeper & sure to hear us.
(so she said)

Suggestive to Visitor
I used nearly a tin of Keating
& between me & you, it was time

I heard the crash. Mum
but I don't know what did it

Everyone has their
own way Mam, but I
always laid it that way at 'ome

51

him. When an aide-de-camp rode up and ordered him back to the lines, the man explained that he was valet to Lord Raglan, the elderly commander-in-chief, and that he was merely taking him his lunch.[21]

In many a big house, the old, devoted retainers still survived in the Victorian age, but they were a dying breed. The penny post, the railways and the growth of newspapers all helped to widen the horizons of servants. Even the greatest lords found that the feudal attraction of their ancestral names was no longer enough to guarantee a lifetime of loyal and respectful service in their employment. 'A short time ago', the Earl of Shaftesbury

A servant of the 'right sort'. Ninety-year-old Ruth Jones who entered service at the age of nineteen photographed in 1912.

told the annual tea meeting of the Female Servants' Home Society in 1877, 'I had a footman—a nice, civil fellow. After a period he wanted to leave, and I asked him the reason. At first he would not answer. At last he said, "I like my Lord's service, but there is no time for me to go to my club".' Such dishonourable desires seem to have offended the sensibilities of the Earl—great social reformer though he was—for he added sanctimoniously: 'Three years afterwards this poor fellow died of consumption, and on his death bed he regretted having left my service.'[22]

Wages were increased significantly in many noble households in the 1860s, but this failed to prevent a certain degeneration in the quality of some of the lower servants, which was lamented as much by faithful retainers as it was by lords. The high life, which had always been a downstairs feature of the big house, when the eagle eye of the housekeeper was turned, became even more common. There was more card playing by the men servants; more frequent visits by the bookmaker's runner from the nearest town; more drunkenness; more pillow fights at night; more carelessness with plates and cups; more practical joking; more petting, and sometimes fornication, in the housemaid's broom cupboard; and much less awe and respect for both upper servants and masters, as a new and untrained class of lower servants was brought in.

In 1830, Mr J Hows, a gentleman who was down on his luck, wrote to Lord Calthorpe about a situation.

I applied on Monday last to Lady Calthorpe and had the honor of an interview with her Ladyship who informed me 'That however competent I might be, yet not having lived in a Situation before, your Lordship was so extremely particular, her Ladyship feared you would object to me.'

But upon the statement of that particularity I have ventured to address your Lordship, hoping by the account I can give of myself and the strong references I can give in point of respectability and character to be enabled to remove your Lordship's scruples and to prevail on your Lordship at least to grant me a trial.

I am 28 years of age, Single, have been in Business but, owing to the pressure of the time, gave it up. My parents are people of property, yet they having a large family I wish to settle myself rather than be an incumbrance upon them.[23]

It seems likely that by the end of Queen Victoria's reign, when many employers had been forced to lower the social barriers downstairs by admitting even tradesmen such as former grocer's assistants to their staffs, the writer of the letter would have had much less difficulty in securing a situation.

Mistresses and Maids

In Victorian times status-conscious individuals were just as quick to count up the number of servants in a house as their modern counterparts are to note the makes of cars outside a house today. There was then no surer way to rise in other people's estimation than to employ a staff of servants larger than most acquaintances thought you could afford, as the total size and composition of the establishment usually provided an immediate guide to the employer's wealth. In 1844 one writer on domestic economy published a table of recommended establishments of servants for various incomes. Only noblemen of high rank and great wealth, he wrote, could afford to maintain first-rate establishments, such as those which have just been described. People with much smaller incomes of £4,500 to £5,000 a year should have an establishment of the second rate, consisting of a butler, who also doubled as house steward, and four other male and nine women servants. In third-rate establishments, suitable for those with incomes of £3,500 to £4,000 a year, the butler also had to act as valet, and there should be only one footman, one under-footman and seven women. Establishments of the fourth rate, where the income was £1,500 to £2,500, should be composed of two men and four women; while the fifth-rate (£1,000 to £1,200) should have only one man-of-all-work and three women. People with incomes of £600 to £700 were advised to content themselves with a sixth-rate establishment of a cook, a housemaid and a footboy, while those with only £450 to £500 a year would have to do without the footboy. An eighth-rate establishment (£250 to £300) should consist of one maidservant and a girl; and the ninth (£150 to £200) of a solitary maid-of-all-work. 'Incomes still less', the writer added, 'will admit of a girl only, or with the occasional use of a charwoman.'[1]

Not everyone accepted his cautious advice, as the pressures not only to keep up with the Joneses but to surpass them, were so great that some ladies starved themselves and members of their family so that they could employ the largest possible staff of servants. There were many real-life parallels to Thackeray's fictional Lady Susan Scraper with her 'jobbed' horses and her young daughters who were reputed to assuage their constant pangs of hunger by eating buns.[2]

One old county family, the Dacres, who lived in Rodney

Street, Liverpool, 'for the sake of combining economy and gaiety, and striving to keep up an appearance of wealth and station upon very small means', were forced to accept numerous privations so that they could employ a footman and a coachman, (both in livery), a cook, a governess, a lady's maid and numerous other servants. Rose Allen, who worked for them in the 1830s, said: 'I never saw a good fire the whole time I was there; no one had sufficient bedding for winter; the bread was often so stale, that it had to be soaked in water before it could be used. . . . The family, when alone, would often live upon heavy puddings to satisfy the cravings of hunger, and every invitation was eagerly

Some servants of Victorian town houses took on all the manners and refinement of their employers.

accepted, to lessen the charges of food, candles and fuel.'[3] The cook and the coachman were bound to the Dacres by long service and large accumulations of unpaid wages; but younger servants, like Rose Allen, left just as quickly as they could.

The Dacres of Liverpool were not unique, but they were exceptional. Most families tried to live more comfortably within their income, which meant that very few could afford to employ that prime status symbol: a man servant. Even if a first-class butler had deigned to work in any home more humble than that of a nobleman's, he would have made such extravagant demands for excellence of food and drink, personal assistance, and the preservation of his own status, that the employer would have soon found himself on the way to Carey Street. To employ a 'single-handed man', as he was curiously called, was rarely a satisfactory substitute. Although this class of servant had not suffered an amputation, the loss of an arm or two would usually have made very little difference to his work, as he was often lazy, drunk or otherwise unwilling or incapable. For these reasons male indoor servants were something of a rarity in middle-class homes; though, during Victorian times, there was a great increase in the numbers outside, with many more gardeners, grooms, coachmen and 'tigers'—young lads, or less frequently, undersized men in livery, who accompanied their employers, when they went out driving, to hold the horse's head when they reached their destination. Apart from these male servants in the grounds and stables, most middle-class families relied on women, a kind of gigantic 'Mum's Army' in their uniform cap and apron, and armed with brooms and feather dusters, which had been assembled to defend the cleanliness and sanctity of the British home and the social honour of the mistress.

By present-day standards, the middling middle classes lived in more than ample accommodation. When Alice Pollock married a lawyer in the Land Registry towards the end of Queen Victoria's reign, they could afford to move on his salary of £750 a year (plus an allowance of £200 from his mother) into a house in Belgrave Road, London, with five bedrooms, a bathroom, a double drawing room, a dining room, a study and a workroom. Mrs Pollock employed the customary trio of servants for such a home: a cook at £20 to £26 a year; a parlourmaid at £16 to £18; and a housemaid at £12 to £14, which was cheap enough as their total wages only consumed 5 to 6 per cent of the Pollocks' total income.[4] To this essential triumvirate, there could be added as the exigencies of birth demanded, or as an increase in income permitted, other servants such as nursemaids, nurses, ladies' maids, kitchenmaids, tweenies (who assisted the housemaid in the morning and the cook in the afternoon) and governesses. The latter, who were very often German girls or the daughters of impoverished clergymen (like Charlotte Brontë), always had a rather ambiguous status, being often too refined to mix easily with the other servants and invariably too poor to be accepted as equals by the daughters of the household.

These two unsophisticated servants from a small, country rectory make a vivid contrast to their city cousins on the previous page.

MRS. MASSEY'S AGENCY FOR SERVANTS, DERBY.

LONDON BRANCH OFFICE: 10, BAKER STREET, PORTMAN SQUARE.	OFFICE HOURS: 10 TO 5. SATURDAY 10 TO 1.	HEAD OFFICE:
TELEPHONE :—5360 & 5361 MAYFAIR TWO LINES. TELEGRAMS:—" SERVANTS," DERBY. "DARBILDEN," LONDON.		101, FRIAR GATE, DERBY.

Nov. 13/12

Particulars of Maid.

-:-:-:-:-:-:-:-:-:-:-:-:-:-:-:-:-:-:-

Emma Reeks,

    C/o Mrs Wright

        Newbrook,

            Atherton,

                Nr Manchester.

with whom she has lived 7 months as maid to two ladies and leaves by her own wish.

      Previously she was 6 months as maid with Mrs Worsley Taylor, Moreton Hall, Whalley, Lancs., and before that she was 2½ years as young ladies maid with the Misses Upcher of Kingham Rectory, Attleboro, and 2½ years as maid with Mrs Herbert Armstrong of Preston.

      Age 26, height 5ft 6½, belongs to the Church of England, is an experienced dressmaker & hairdresser a good plain needlewoman, good packer, free November 20th and he home is in Cambs. I have told her the wages offered.

-:-:-:-:-:-:-:-:-:-:-:-:-:-:-:-:-:-:-

Story of a Life. Particulars of a maid as presented by an Agency for servants in 1912.

A young girl, who wanted, or needed, to enter service, often obtained a local, part-time job first to save up for her uniform. Although some employers, like Alice Pollock, provided the formal black afternoon dress, frilly apron and white cap free of charge, most mistresses did not do so. Girls had to buy their own caps and aprons, their formal and working dresses of blue or pink cotton, and other necessary clothing, which cost in all some £4 or £5, a considerable sum of money for a working-class girl in those days. Some charities helped poor girls of good character, by providing them with a complete outfit, the debt being paid off by regular deductions from their wages. Through buying wholesale, charities were able to reduce the total cost to under £3, which in 1884 provided two chemises, two pairs of drawers, two flannel petticoats, one top petticoat, one pair of stays, two nightdresses, two print dresses, one stuff dress, four coarse aprons, four white aprons, two pairs of stockings, one pair of boots, one hat, one jacket, a pair of slippers and 'a good, stout box' to contain them.[5]

There were a number of different ways in which the girl might obtain her first full-time situation. In the country, the Church of England acted as one of the biggest unofficial recruitment agencies, with vicars and their wives sifting and certifying suitable candidates. During church services, with their forty-minute sermons, ladies from local big houses would often break off from their pious meditations to run a sharp, appraising eye over the young girls in the congregation, to seek out likely looking recruits for their own household staffs, who might be favoured later by an exploratory visit from a servant emissary. In the big cities, tradesmen, with their inside knowledge of local houses, often advised servants of vacancies, sometimes in the hope that their help might be remembered later if any changes were made in those who provided goods or services for the household. Their advice, however, was not infallible. On the recommendation of a Knightsbridge shopkeeper, Mary Ann Ashford went to a doctor's house in Great Sloane Street, London, to inquire about a vacancy for a cook; but she was saved in the nick of time, just as she was about to ring the bell, when a better-informed cheesemonger came up the area steps and warned her: 'You may as well live with Old Nick as come here, for they have had four cooks in three months.'[6] Recommendations from friends who were already in service were another common means of obtaining a place. Failing that, a girl could scan the advertisement columns of a county or a national newspaper, or make inquiries at a registry office, though some of these, as we shall see, were no more than baits set for unwary girls by brothel-keepers and white-slave traffickers.

Young girls rarely knew what to expect in their first situation, though it usually did not take them very long to find out. Whether they would find happiness or not depended to a very great extent on the character of the mistress; some were incapable of dealing with staff and suffered great mental and emotional anguish themselves in their inadequate attempts to do so. This could happen even in aristocratic houses, where relationships between mistresses and maids were governed by firmly established traditions, strict conventions and unwritten rules. (Remember Lady Spencer and the tennis court!) Although the housekeeper, who was much more of a terrifying figure to maids, could take many burdens off her mistress, the latter could not escape all responsibilities, and there must have been many, like Lady Frederick Cavendish, who lived in the hell of her own self-acknowledged incompetence:

London, May 17th, 1865 The kitchen-maid turns out sick and incapable; the upper-housemaid pert, fine and lazy. Woe is me!
Chatsworth, November 7th, 1866 It perplexes me sadly how all I say and do, though it is not without prayer, seems to fail utterly with one maid after another.

Chatsworth, December 4th, 1866 I am shivering all over with a miserable scene with my maid who squabbles with all the servants.

Chatsworth, December 12th, 1866 To my inexpressible relief and comfort, my odious little maid went off, and gentle, pleasant-looking quiet little Mrs Parry came, who will probably turn out a Felon, but is meanwhile very soothing.[7]

These were private thoughts confided to a diary; in public most aristocrats usually preserved a stiff upper lip in their dealings with servants—and with much else! Some of them could certainly be haughty and demanding, but it seems that middle-class mistresses were usually worse. These new ladies had no aristocratic reticence. They were paying and they intended to

Many young boys were employed in Victorian households as pages (left) and 'tigers' (right), who accompanied their masters or mistresses while they were out driving.

get their money's worth. Rose Allen recalled how she applied in the 1830s for the post of lady's maid to a Mrs Bennet who lived in the Liverpool suburb of Aigburth. After a lengthy walk to the house and a wait of ten minutes in a cold, draughty corridor, Rose was told by another servant that Mrs Bennet was just not in the mood to see her then, but she could call again the following day. The next day, after another ten-minute wait (just to show who was boss), Rose was shown into the drawing room, where Mrs Bennet was spread out on one side of the fireplace, nursing a fat, overfed poodle on her lap, while Mr Bennet was sitting opposite her, with a gouty leg propped up. After Mrs Bennet had asked Rose a multitude of questions about herself, her family and her previous situations, discussing the answers with her husband as if no one else was in the room, Rose asked what her duties would be.

'Nothing heavy', Mrs Bennet replied. 'There's my old china in this room, in my bedroom and in the closet, which must be dusted every day: there's breakfast for the dog, cat and parrot; indeed, all the meals you would have to prepare; and my dear poodle can't eat meat unless it's nicely minced. They must be washed every other day and combed every day; and the poodle must go for a walk when it is sunshiny, only you must never let him wet his feet, but carry him across the streets. They must sleep in your room, as I should not feel easy for them to be left alone. Then there's my caps; you would wash and make them, and I always change them three times a week. Of course, you would have to attend my toilet; but that would not take long, as I am never more than an hour morning and evening, and two hours before dinner. You can write, I suppose?'

'Yes, Ma'am.'

'I should want you to write always to tradespeople, and invitation notes for my whist parties. Do you like reading?'

'Yes, Ma'am, very much.'

'I don't know, then, whether you'll suit me. The last maid liked reading, and she kept my poor Polly waiting for his supper twice in one month; and sometimes she forgot to wash the cat on Mondays, Wednesdays and Fridays, and would do it on Tuesdays or Thursdays, which I never can permit.'

When Rose discovered that she was also expected to sit with Mr Bennet through his attacks of gout and to act as the target for his abuse and the occasional hurled book or slipper, she wisely decided to decline the post. As she left the room, she heard Mrs Bennet say to her husband: 'Really girls are so saucy in these days, there's no bearing it.'[8]

Complaints by middle-class mistresses became more strident and more frequent as the years passed. Servants were showered with advice, abuse and admonitions. Dozens of books were published, hundreds of pamphlets were printed, and thousands of sermons were preached in an attempt to mould servants to their mistress's will. Christianity was pressed into secular service: texts commanding obedience (Eph 6:5; Col 3:22; Titus 2:9; 1 Pet 2:18) were liberally quoted. One of the most popular preachers among middle-class Londoners was the Rev. W B Mackenzie, of St James's Church, Holloway, who proclaimed that it was the duty of every servant to have 'profound reverence for your superiors, submission under your trials, and a spirit of thankful contentment with your lot'.[9] Mistresses, but not maids, thought he was wonderful and worshipped his very words. The Religious Tract Society published homilies on such texts as, 'She looketh well to the ways of her household, and eateth not the bread of idleness.'[10] Not to be outdone, the Society for Promoting Christian Knowledge published its own books of advice, of which the following is fully representative:

Don't think too much about wages; serving in 'a safe, happy home is of greater consequence'.

Don't deny faults in a 'saucy indignant way'. If something has been lost, offer to have your own possessions searched.

Don't gossip with tradespeople or servants.

Don't get into a temper if the hall or the steps you have just cleaned are immediately spattered with mud by thoughtless people.

Don't read 'silly sensational stories' in 'poisonous publications which are brought to the back doors of gentlemen's homes'.

Don't let candles 'flare away for hours without being of use'.

Remember to pray carefully and regularly.[11]

Christianity was given a utilitarian tinge. One woman writer told how a servant had been so greatly changed by her

Working life started at a very early age for maids in 1860.

conversion that she had actually started to sweep under the mats. 'That', the author added sanctimoniously, 'was practical Christianity.'[12] A far more subtle approach was employed in this great Victorian propaganda campaign by the author of *Hints to Young Women about to enter Service,* who tried to disarm readers first by freely admitting that domestic service was naturally repugnant to everyone. 'The pride of our heart rebels against being servants—we would all of us rather be masters; but rest assured of this, that we can never be truly happy or comfortable in this world, till God gives us grace not only to submit to the position in which He has placed us, but to be heartily contented and thankful for it.'[13] These perversions of the Christian message helped to destroy many young servants' faith in the Church and its teachings so that as the Rev. Mackenzie admitted in 1851—the year of the first nation-wide religious census—there was a 'growing but most distressing deception' among some young servant girls, like that of Gehazi or Ananias, 'a monstrous crime' which 'mocks the all-seeing God'—of only pretending to go to Church on Sundays.[14]

Some mistresses did face a most difficult task with their young charges. These country girls arrived in London and other big cities, their ambitions inflamed by fantastic visions of sophisticated romance and long hours of leisure, implanted by their servant friends, only to find that their dreams had to be compressed into one day's brief excursion after a month's or six weeks' unending drudgery, and perhaps a short evening break once a week. They were often inexperienced in domestic work, uneducated and resentful of authority. Torn away abruptly from their friends and family at the start of life, they felt displaced and lonely. The late hours of work, the excesses of heat in the underground kitchens and of cold in the attic bedrooms, and the long hours of close confinement made them tired and irritable, faded their fresh country complexions, and sometimes so irreparably weakened their constitutions that tuberculosis and heart disease were a consequence. They were unable to accept the negative life that service entailed with 'no followers, no friends in the kitchen, no laughing to be heard above stairs, no romping for young girls to whom romping is an instinct all the same as with lambs and kittens, no cessation of work except at meal times, no getting out for half an hour into the bright sunshine save "on the sly" or after the not always pleasant process of asking leave.'[15] Some girls were tempted into theft by their employer's abundant wealth and more than adequate opportunity: thefts by servants accounted for the largest total loss of property in the Metropolitan Police area in 1837.[16] Pilfering of less valuable items was even more common. According to Mr Philip Holdsworth, a former Marshal of the City of London, old linen and bottles and similar items could be easily sold to the numerous chandler's shops and green stalls in the capital.[17]

There were many false hopes and expectations on both sides of the green baize door. Some middle-class mistresses genuinely

The countryside was scoured for new recruits to service. Hundreds of thousands of girls left their families and homes to work in the cities and towns.

believed themselves to be involved in a vast educational project, a levelling-up process which would elevate their own daughters into ladies and transform their servants into ladies' maids at least. But they did not consult; they tried to impose their beliefs. Their excessive zeal and self-righteousness made them imperious: 'I allow no answers', was the ever-ready rebuke on their lips. But mistresses' attitudes to servants were equivocal. Although they wanted them to be lady-like, they did not want them to be ladies, a fundamental ambiguity which was revealed in the contrasting attitudes towards dress and speech.

In aggregate, mistresses must have spent millions of hours, literally, in trying to refine their servants' speech into an acceptable, but often no more correct, middle-class norm. The following table was intended to instruct ladies' maids specifically; but most mistresses would undoubtedly have felt that all other kinds of servants could have derived equivalent benefit from it.

Vulgar	Correct
Close the door	Shut the door
Below your clothes	Under your clothes
I feel, or find, a smell	I smell
Half six o'clock	Half-past five
She misguides her clothes	She abuses or sullies her clothes
Monday first	Monday next
I got it for half nothing	I got it very cheap
Give me a clean plate	Give me a plate
The child roars	The child cries
Up the stair	Up stairs
Cheese and bread	Bread and cheese[18]

Servants were also instructed in the pronunciation of historic family names such as Home and Cholmondeley, even though they would rarely encounter them outside the pages of their mistress's copy of Burke's *Peerage*, which was second only in popularity to the Bible as the favourite occasional-table book. Fresh from the study of their own books of advice, mistresses

Mistresses often complained of the lack of education among servants. The caption read:
Miss Rose (who has kindly taken in hand an illiterate housemaid): 'Five and one make six. That's right. Now what do one and six make?'
Jane (promptly): 'Eight'n pence Miss.'

would inform their servants that Marjoribanks was pronounced Marshbanks; Mainwaring, Mannering; Meux, Mews; Cockburn, Coburn; Cholmondeley, Chumley; Blyth, Bly; Waldegrave, Walgrave; Strachan, Strawn; Gower, Gor; Home, Hume; Tollemache, Tollmash; Bethune, Beeton; Glamis, Glams; and Bicester, Bister.[19] Pronunciation marked social frontiers; the aspiring middle classes, often only a generation removed from the class below, took enormous delight in jokes about 'hignorant' servants speaking what became known as Cockney Domestic:

> *Lady:* Wish to leave! Why, I thought, Thompson, you were very comfortable with me!
> *Thompson (who is extremely refined):* Ho, yes, mum! I don't find no fault with you, mum—nor yet with master—but the truth *his*, mum—the *hother* servants is so 'orrid vulgar and hignorant, and speaks so hungrammatical, that I reely cannot live in the same 'ouse with 'em.[20]

It was little wonder that such jokes, which reinforced the middle-class sense of superiority, should have become mainstays of *Punch* and similar compilations; but the jokes turned sour when the mistress's own children started to copy the servants' 'hignorant' speech.

Ladies' fears that their children might be infected not only socially but also physically by contact with the servants made them insist on cleanliness of both person and appearance. Bad smells, which in pre-Pasteur days were believed to be carriers of disease, were a great problem in many Victorian houses, owing to the frequent proximity of kitchen and dining room; the scarcity of baths, particularly for servants; the ubiquitous chamber pots; the inefficient drainage systems; the lack of disposable sanitary towels, which were not manufactured until Edwardian times; and the attitudes of country girls towards personal hygiene. It was not unusual for some young servant girls to wear the same thick stockings for a week at a time and to wash their feet only once a month. This was apparently so common that the *Servants' Magazine* found it necessary to publish an article 'Beware of the Feet', which advised that 'the feet should be washed daily, as well as the armpits, from which an offensive odour is also emitted, unless daily ablution is practised. Cleanliness is next to godliness.'[21]

Some mistresses went in such great dread of dirt and infection that, like Mrs Tayton of Bromley, Kent, they refused to allow their servants to bring their boxes into the house 'for fear of being overrun with importations of London bugs.'[22] The mere mention of the word was enough to give most ladies palpitations, as bugs, being no respecters of social class, could easily breach the defences of their closely guarded temples of propriety and cleanliness. The *Servants' Magazine* published an involved and alarming calculation showing that one bug could produce in the course of a single year no less than twenty-two million others and

George Cruikshank's satirical view of
the hardships of downstairs life.
Toasting themselves before the fire in
1847 are (from left to right) the cook,
footman, housemaid and page.

added gravely: 'If a knowledge of this fact will not induce
activity among servants to extirpate the first bug which makes its
appearance in a dwelling, we do not know what will.'[23]
Domestic encyclopaedias published many different remedies,
including brushing spirits of naphtha into every part of the
bedstead and using a poison made up of camphor, oil of
turpentine and corrosive sublimate, a practice which may have
caused no fewer sleepless nights than bugs among the nervous.

Although mistresses wanted their servants to be as clean and
as neat as ladies, they were equally adamant that their clothes
should immediately indicate their true station in life. In earlier
times, the middle classes themselves had been prevented from
wearing gold-threaded samite robes and silken camlet cloaks by
the sumptuary laws; now they, in their turn, imposed similar
restrictions on their servants, which they were expected to obey
even in their few short hours of leisure. The author of one article,

'Friendly Hints on Dress', stipulated that 'a gown should never be made in that Fashion which is suitable only for mistresses; a profusion of ribbons on the cap and flowers in the bonnet are out of character; long drop earrings are likewise very unseemly.'[24] One mistress tried to prove that it was legitimate for ladies to wear fine silks and jewels because it encouraged trade; and in case that partial economic argument failed, she fell back on the old prop of Christianity, warning servants—but not mistresses— to 'think of the morning of the Resurrection, and how utterly base and insignificant all this world's vanities will seem to us then.'[25] These new sumptuary laws were as bitterly resented by servants as the equally stringent rules that no 'followers' should be brought into the house. Their attempts to evade this high-handed interference in their personal life also laid the basis for a stock, middle-class joke, which was repeated with innumerable variations. One version went:

> A mistress ran short of change one day and called down the kitchen stairs: 'May, have you any coppers down there?' The reply was : 'Yes, ma'am, but they are both my cousins.'[26]

Domestic service was never popular with women from the start. Apologists like John Duguid Milne might claim that 'with abundant work, it combines a wonderful degree of liberty, discipline, health, physical comfort, good example, regularity, room for advancement, encouragement to acquire saving habits', but few servants would have believed him.[27] When there were other opportunities for employment, they were eagerly seized. In spite of all the disadvantages, Lancashire girls preferred to work in cotton mills, where the rates of pay were higher (about £23 a year for a girl of sixteen to twenty-one in the 1830s); the hours of work no longer; and, even more important, the sense of personal freedom and independence, much greater. As a consequence, domestic servants were so scarce in Lancashire that, according to one official report of 1840, 'they can only be obtained from the neighbouring counties.'[28] Contrary to much popular belief, it was servants who were despised among the working classes, not factory girls. One servant, the daughter of a licensed victualler, found that she had 'lost caste' among her own relations by going into service; when she was in their home and anyone came in, 'I was requested to step into another room, and kept in the background.'[29]

There were far too many inadequate, inconsiderate and domineering mistresses chasing too few well-trained, willing servants. The faithful old servant was not entirely a myth, particularly in the country, but she was much rarer than we think. Even in the best-run households, with the most considerate employers, there was a constant coming and going among the staff, with important posts such as that of parlourmaid, often remaining vacant for months, or even years, until a suitable candidate presented herself. Mary Frances Hardcastle, of Adelaide Crescent, Brighton, Sussex, was

The difficulty of finding servants became a stock joke of middle-class drawing rooms. 'We never have any trouble getting servants,' said the hostess, 'we've had ten different ones in the last month.'

obviously in her younger days a fair and reasonable mistress who rewarded efficient service with increases of pay; but even she was unable to retain the majority of her servants for long. A few, like Mary Bound, remained in her employment as a housemaid for seventeen years from 1867 to 1884, when she left to be married; while Frances Marlow came as a nurserymaid at £7 a year in 1864 and left in 1876 (also to marry) by which time she had become a £20-a-year lady's maid to the daughters who were then grown up. But most of the other four or five servants on the staff did not stay long, leaving for a variety of reasons of which illness, death, marriage, 'not being equal to the situation', and better jobs in other households were the most important.[30]

The turnover of staff in some other houses was even greater. The servants' account book of Vice-Admiral Sir Henry Shiffner, kept between the years of 1832 and 1845, reads in places more like a court martial roll than a simple record of civilian engagements and dismissals. In 1839 the cook was sacked for being 'extravagant' and a kitchenmaid for being 'a dirty insolent girl with a very great lack of truth'. Two more cooks were dismissed in 1840, one for being 'troublesome' and the other for being 'fond of drink' (a common fault among cooks) and 'a very moderate *artiste*' (also common); while a lady's maid 'with a light regard for truth', a kitchen maid, who was 'dirty and of doubtful honesty', and a laundry maid—'maddish, methinks'—were also sent packing.[31] Domestic service could have brought little pleasure and few benefits to either maids or mistresses in such a household.

Only in Britain, did middle-class mistresses with limited incomes but excessive social aspirations try to create a snobbish replica of the great lord's establishment in their far more modest homes. No English mistress would have tolerated the French servant's familiarity, or the informality of dinner when the *bonne* would come straight into the dining room from the kitchen carrying the steaming dish of succulent food that she had just cooked. 'The English servant', wrote Fenimore Cooper, 'will not bear familiarity, scarcely kindness; the Frenchman will hardly dispense with both.'[32] In the English colonies, mistresses commonly worked with their servants at the household chores, just as their ancestors had done in the eighteenth century; while in the United States two servants would have been considered sufficient for a childless couple living in a three-or four-storey brown-stone front in New York.[33]

The English lack of labour-saving devices, the insistence on household perfection, the emphasis on status, which was reflected in the kitchen where the professed cook insisted on having her own kitchenmaid, meant that the size of staff, though not the total wage bill, was very often twice as big in Britain than it would have been elsewhere. In the following chapter we shall see what these large staffs of servants were expected to do—and not to do—in Victorian middle-class homes.

Up With the Lark!

One of the few frivolous exhibits at the 1851 Great Exhibition in the Crystal Palace, London, was a specially-designed bedstead for servants, incorporating an automatic clockwork device which, at the appointed hour, withdrew a support from the foot of the bed so that it collapsed and threw the occupant onto the floor. This bedstead remained a prototype, a caprice of the fertile British imagination and inventiveness, but it must have brought many a supercilious smile to the lips of lady visitors for whom the laziness of servants had become proverbial. It is easier for us, than it was for them, to understand why servants were reluctant to leave their beds at dawn; to dress in a cold, draughty room; to creep down the stairs for fear of waking the master and the mistress; and to enter a cold kitchen where the range had to be blackleaded and the hearth whitened before a kettle could be boiled; particularly as some dinner party or other celebration on the previous night might have kept them busily occupied until 10 o'clock in washing up other people's greasy plates and scouring sticky saucepans. That, after all, is not the sort of job which suits everyone.

Lower servants had to get up with the lark at 5 a.m. or 6 a.m., with a concessionary half-hour's deferment in the winter months, and to start work not many minutes later, two hours or more before they could sit down to their own meagre breakfast. The first to appear was often the little kitchenmaid, who could have been earning as little as two shillings a week, or eight shillings at the most, or the tweeny, who got a few pence less. The first task of the day was to clean and then to light the kitchen range, a most tiresome task especially at that time in the morning. Ranges came in two main varieties: bright and black. Bright stoves had large areas of polished steel which had to be kept as bright as a mirror by liberal applications of rotten-stone and sweet oil and fierce rubbing with a leather. They usually had an alternative set of steel fire-bars for summer use, which were preserved from rust during the winter months (when cast-iron bars were used) by smearing them with mutton fat and wrapping them in brown paper.

To clean the more common cast-iron stove was no less demanding a task. The maid had to place a piece of cloth or old carpet in front of the stove before she raked out the cinders and

swept the dust off the bars, the hobs and the hearth. She then broke off a piece of black lead from a solid block and mixed it with a little water in a small pan so that she could apply it with a round-headed brush to every part of the range. (Wellington black lead cost 1d to 4d a block at one of London's biggest manufacturers, John Oakey and Sons, of Westminster Bridge Road, who also sold a superior liquid product, Brunswick and Berlin Black 'for beautifying and preserving stoves and all kinds of iron work' at 6d to two shillings a bottle.) When the black lead had dried, it was rubbed until it gleamed with a special polishing brush, with a little splay of bristles at the top for getting into the awkward crevices in the ornamental work. Once a week, the flues had to be swept clean of accumulated soot.

Housemaids also rose at 5 a.m. or 6 a.m. and went straight into their strange daily routine of scattering damp tea leaves or wet sand over the carpets, to lay the dust, before they swept them. The main reception rooms and the front hall had to be thoroughly cleaned, dusted and tidied before the family came down to breakfast and, in winter, the grates had to be blackleaded and cheerful fires ablaze. Meanwhile, in larger establishments, the nurserymaid would be busily occupied in the children's suite at the top of the house, sweeping and cleaning the day nursery and lighting the fire.

The upper servants—the cook, the lady's maid, the parlourmaid and that great British gift to upper- and middle-class reminiscences, the nurse, or nanny—often got up an hour or so later, as servant status had to be preserved even in modest establishments. The cook sometimes had the prerogative of early-morning tea in bed, which was brought to her by the kitchenmaid, though this privilege was scarcely paralleled during the rest of her long working day when she would be fully occupied in preparing four different meals of three different kinds for the adults, the children and the servants in the household. Parlourmaids, who were increasingly employed as cut-price substitutes for butlers during Queen Victoria's reign, also had a leisurely start to their long day. They set the table in the dining room, or in the breakfast room in more imposing houses, and sometimes helped to clean the room as well. The lady's maid also had little to do until she woke her mistress with a cup of tea at 8 a.m. Where a mistress could not afford to employ her own personal maid, these duties were performed by the parlourmaid or a housemaid.

Nanny, too, was often a lie-abed, especially if she had been unscrupulous enough to smear the teat of the baby's porcelain bottle with laudanum on the previous night, so that it would sleep on through the first two of the seven mandatory feeds— and, sometimes, unhappily, for ever. Not all middle-class women fed their own babies, despite one male writer's assurance that 'your bosoms' are 'no less charming for having a dear little cherub at your breast.'[1] Many mothers were unable to breast-feed their babies through illness, inability, or sometimes, sheer

Before a kettle could be boiled a fire had to be started. The first chore of the day for the housemaid.

75

repugnance, which in some cases appears to have been just as strong to babies as it was to the intercourse that kept on producing them regularly year after year. Most upper-class and many middle-class women abandoned their babies and their children almost entirely to the care of the nanny, apart from a formal encounter of half an hour or so before or after tea, or a briefer meeting at some other time of the day to inflict a light punishment such as that used by Lady Lyttleton in the 1840s of putting her children's fingers in a letter press and then tightening the screw.[2] Other mothers used even more excruciating punishments. The interest in the refinements of child torture

Reclining in luxury, these two Victorian mistresses are complaining of the way nursemaids neglect their children. '. . . one can't look after one's own children, you know!'

among these outwardly respectable, but inwardly frustrated, middle-class mothers, was so great that the *Englishwoman's Domestic Magazine*—founded by Mrs Beeton's husband— thought it worthwhile to issue a special supplement in 1870 on the whipping of young girls and other forms of punishment.

Many of the children were so starved of affection that they turned to their nurses as a mother-substitute, which certainly explains the high respect in which they were held, and, possibly, much else in Victorian life. Although the police court columns of the newspapers were full of stories of babies being drugged to death by opium, and others being suffocated by the teat of a bottle which had been left in their mouth throughout the night, most nurses (who were the keepers of their mistresses' lost consciences) accepted their special responsibilities conscientiously and ruled their miniature worlds with firmness but with kindness too.

Their first task of the day was to bath and feed the babies, sometimes with a mixture of milk and barley water, and to give the prescribed medicines and purges of castor oil, magnesia, peppermint and senna, which were administered from the age of

An idealised view of the life of a nurserymaid as presented by the *Servants' Magazine* which was designed to keep servants in their proper station.

THE
SERVANTS' MAGAZINE.

No. 29. New Series.]   May 1, 1869.   [Price One Penny.

PLEASING MANNERS OF LOIS.   [See Page 100.

THE GIRL'S OWN PAPER

VOL. VIII.—No. 358.]   NOVEMBER 6, 1886.   [PRICE ONE PENNY.

MERLE'S CRUSADE.

By ROSA NOUCHETTE CAREY, Author of "Aunt Diana," "For Lilias," etc,

CHAPTER V.
MRS. GARNETT'S ROCKERS.

I HAD plenty of time for such intro-spective thoughts as these during my brief railway journey, and before my luggage and I were safely deposited at 35, Queen's Gate.

"I WAS UNDRESSING THE BOY BY THE BEDROOM FIRE."

one month. Although few babies by then were wrapped up entirely in swaddling clothes, like a flannel parcel, some physicians still recommended that a tight binder should be put around the stomach, and be worn in cold or damp weather, until the child had cut its second teeth. Many doctors were also opposed to the modern pram, which first appeared in the second half of the century, so that nurses had to carry the child when they took it out in the mornings and afternoons—until it could walk. The older children were bathed and dressed: little boys were laced up in stays until about the age of seven or eight, and girls went on wearing them for life. Breakfast, which was served at 8 a.m., was usually a spartan meal of porridge or bread and milk with, perhaps, an egg on Sundays: a real third-world contrast to the more than ample breakfast that the adults gorged an hour later.

Just as the nursery was sitting down to its meagre breakfast, the housemaids were carrying cans of hot water, and trays of early morning tea and thin bread and butter, to still recumbent adults in their bedrooms. The lady's maid helped her mistress to dress, a necessary task in an age when women wore tightly laced stays or corsets; many petticoats; steel-hooped crinolines or later horsehair bustles; long drawers or tight pantaloons; and dresses which could contain as much as forty-eight yards of material. In a few households the parlourmaid was expected to valet the master of the house. Parlourmaids, like footmen, were carefully selected for their height and their fine appearance. Some masters were so overcome by early-morning passion when they found a long-legged, good-looking girl, in a cap with coloured streamers, bending over them, that their self-control, which was not always very great, snapped entirely, with natural consequences. Parlourmaids were favourite domestic targets for unfaithful husbands. After Edward Sellon, a former Indian Army officer, had stayed in his bedroom on the pretext of having a headache, his wife found the parlourmaid's cap in his bed, which must have taken some explaining.[3]

Just after eight o'clock all the servants (apart from the nursery staff) sat down at the kitchen table for their breakfast. The tea was poured out by the cook, who also carved slices of meat off the previous day's roast or cut up a cold meat pie, which was all the food most servants had, except, sometimes, for a slice of bread. About three-quarters of an hour later, the parlourmaid beat the gong in the front hall to summon the family, the children, and the servants to family prayers in the dining room, with its ritual five-minute reading from the Bible and its celebration of man's and woman's equality in the sight of God, after which the barriers separating the three worlds were wound up again until the following day. This dishonest ceremony became less common as the reign progressed.

Previously, the parlourmaid had laid the table with a spotless linen cloth; set each place with knives and forks and a table napkin folded into the shape of a mitre; placed bread, rolls, toast,

The *Girl's Own Paper* played its part in preparing young girls for lives as devoted servants.

butter dishes, jars of jam and whole honeycombs in the middle of the table and, at the top, a cream jug, a sugar basin and a suitable number of cups and saucers. When the prayers were over, she brought in the breakfast dishes and put them on the sideboard or on a side table covered with a white cloth.

The Victorians liked their food in great quantities (if they were rich enough to afford it) and there were usually two or three hot dishes, selected from bacon and eggs, kidneys, cutlets, broiled chicken, omelette or fish, according to the taste and the opulence of the household; and, in wealthier houses, there was often an additional choice of cold dishes, such as ham, tongue,

'Ronuk' supplied the polish but the poor maid had to supply the elbow grease to create the mirror-like floor.

game pie and potted meat. In aristocratic circles, it had become fashionable for the family to help themselves to breakfast, without the aid of the servants, who were banished from the room, and, as Henry James observed in 1877, 'accordingly, through the length and breadth of England, everyone who has the slightest pretension to standing high enough to feel the way the social breeze is blowing' conforms, even though the custom involved 'a vast amount of leaning and stretching, of waiting and perambulating.'[4] When the meal was over, the parlourmaid cleared the table and washed up.

While the members of the family were gorging, the housemaids had turned their attentions to the upstairs rooms, with their rumpled beds, their dirty baths and washbasins, their full chamberpots, and their trails of rejected clothing. The strategy for cleaning a bedroom—and every other room—had been formulated in countless books and articles with an attention to detail which would not have discredited Clausewitz. Housemaids were instructed to fling open the windows to air the room, not forgetting first to lay all swing mirrors on their backs, so that they would not be blown over and broken in the draught. The bedclothes had to be pulled back and draped over two chairs which had been thoughtfully placed at the foot of the bed already. The portable hip baths had to be carried away and emptied and the washbasins also had to be emptied and cleaned. One of the housemaids' most distasteful tasks was to empty the chamberpots. They had to be covered with a cloth and carried discreetly down the back stairs (which were also used for coffins) to avoid offending the susceptibilities of the very people who had filled them. When they had been emptied, they had to be scoured clean and wiped.

To make a Victorian bed was neither a short nor a simple task. There were usually three mattresses. The heavy bottom mattress, stuffed with straw, was turned only once a week; the middle mattress, made of wool or horsehair, was turned daily; and the feather mattress on top had to be shaken, pummelled, smacked and turned every day until it was free from all unpleasant lumps and as light and puffed up as a soufflé.

Every square inch of the carpets had to be swept clean; all the fittings, furniture and ornaments had to be thoroughly dusted; and every pane of glass and mirror had to be polished until they shone. Once a fortnight, the carpets were rolled up and carried downstairs to be beaten. Deal floors were scrubbed clean with soap and water to which a little potassium carbonate was added to give a finish of unblemished purity, even though it would not be seen once the carpets had been replaced. Oak floors were polished with beeswax, which was often procured from the apiary in the grounds or garden. Constant kneeling laid many maids low with their occupational disease of housemaid's knee, a chronic inflammation of the knee-cap; but one mistress was still able to recommend scrubbing as 'good healthy exercise' even though it is certain that she had never tried it herself.[5] But

A 'simple' bedroom as supplied by
Messrs. Jackson and Graham, 84
Oxford Street, London, in 1880.

Victorian mistresses were born, not to work, but to command.

At 11 a.m. work was briefly interrupted for a tea-break in the kitchen, but the poor housemaids were soon down on their knees again, scrubbing away in a fury of suds and lather to keep up with the aristocratic schedule which decreed that their work had to be finished by midday. Meanwhile, the mistress had consulted with the cook over the menus of the day, making any suggestions

82

which lay within the bounds of her imagination or the limits of her cook's toleration, as many were so jealous of their professional competence that they resented much interference in their kitchen.

The servants had their *dinner*, in contrast to the family's *lunch*, between midday and one o'clock. If the cook was busy, drunk, or just plain indifferent, it might be a cold meal again, but more often it consisted of roast and vegetables, followed by a rice or suet pudding, or an apple pie or treacle tart. In some households beer was served, or an allowance of one shilling a week, was given in its place. The nursery sometimes had the same meal as the kitchen, but very often they were given something more economical, such as shepherd's pie or mutton broth, while, once again, the adults fared the best.

In aristocratic circles, luncheon was a semi-social affair, which older children were permitted to attend. The meal, which was served *à la Russe* by liveried footmen, could include such rare delicacies as speckled blue plover's eggs in their original nests, as Harriet Beecher Stowe discovered when she lunched with the Duke and Duchess of Sutherland at their London home. This dish aroused such vivid recollections of a robin's nest in her own orchard at home that she could not bring herself to touch it.[6]

Although the cuisine was less elaborate and the livery was absent, the middle classes tried to create a counterfeit presentation of the same event in their own homes. The parlourmaid, who had by then exchanged her cotton frock for a more formal black dress, laid each place at the table with two large knives and forks, claret and sherry glasses, and table napkins. The cold sweets, such as jellies, creams, pastries and dishes of fruit for dessert were put in the centre of the table, as middle-class luncheons were not usually served *à la Russe*. 'It is needless to say', wrote A Member of the Aristocracy 'that table-mats, or slips, as they are vulgarly termed, are as inadmissible at luncheon as at dinner or breakfast.'[7] The same writer also recommended that the parlourmaid should not announce the meal with the butler's stock phrase of 'Luncheon is served', as that would sound pretentious; instead she should use a more homely and concrete phrase such as 'Luncheon is on the table, ma'am.'[8]

The ladies, still wearing their outdoor clothes, would then walk ceremoniously into the dining room, two by two, like animals entering the Ark, followed by any gentlemen who were sufficiently well versed in etiquette to know that it would be most improper for them to take a lady's arm as they did at dinner, for if they had, it would have revealed them as vulgar impostors, and not true gentlemen. At the table, the ladies would take off their fur wraps and winter cloaks, unpeel their gloves and throw up their veils (which might otherwise have been somewhat restrictive of feeding), but they would keep their bonnets firmly on as aristocratic ladies also did. Luncheon was served by the parlourmaid. There was often a simple entrée, such as *saumon*

Dinner below stairs in a great house. 1902.

Dressing the lady of the house became almost a problem of structural engineering in Victorian England.

mayonnaise followed by a choice of hot dishes—beef, chicken or lamb—and after that a pudding or a sweet, and finally fresh fruit for dessert.

Although the Victorians had big appetites they did not linger long over their meals, which may account for some of their more dyspeptic views and attitudes. Within half an hour or so, they would be back again in the drawing room, fidgeting with their bonnets and drawing on their gloves, prior to their departure, which was made no more than twenty minutes after the meal had ended. Coffee or tea was never served at luncheon, as no lady could have afforded to delay her equally compelling social obligations, which started at about 2.30 p.m., with the leaving of cards, or at 3 p.m. with ceremonious visits to acquaintances, which were still anachronistically described as 'morning calls', as they had been in the previous century, even though they had by then been transferred to the afternoon.

At Home

Caller: 'Is Mrs Brown at home?'
Artless Parlourmaid: (smiling
Confidentially)
'No Ma'am—she really *is* out this
afternoon.'

Unless Victorian ladies were in mourning or indisposed (two events which occurred with regrettable regularity), they often devoted the remainder of their day to a vertiginous round of social engagements, which were governed by conventions of Byzantine complexity. Propriety was maintained just as strictly among ladies as it was between mistress and maid. Precedence was guarded as closely as the Crown jewels, and rank was defined with tortuous exactitude. One very popular writer on etiquette found it necessary to make a subtle distinction between the 'great little' and the 'little great': the former being the professional and mercantile classes and the latter, the '*old*, solid COUNTY PEOPLE, the descendants of patrician families, the Squirearchy'.[1] All people, of whatever rank, were expected to know their place; if anyone had the temerity to forget it, he or she was publicly reminded. At county balls, for instance, the upper end of the hall was sometimes reserved for the exclusive use of the 'little great' by a heavy red and gilt cord; but more frequently, their territory was more intangibly protected by the snub or the 'cut', of which the Victorians were supreme masters—and mistresses.

Similar conventions governed the esoteric mysteries of the afternoon. In the metropolis, great ladies would drive off in their four-wheeled coaches, attended by a pair of flamboyantly attired footmen, who would inquire of the equally resplendent footman, hall porter or butler if the mistress of the house was at home. If she were in residence, the lady would enter; otherwise, she would give her footman three cards to leave, one of her own for the mistress of the house and two of her husband's for the mistress and the master.

The afternoon ritual was basically the same in the suburbs, other large cities and provincial towns. After luncheon, middle-class ladies, freshly washed, and brushed up by their lady's maid if they had one, would set out with tight-lipped determination and fluttering hopes to make their round of calls on foot or in a carriage: these visits would determine almost entirely the fullness of their own and their husband's social life during the coming weeks. 'Card leaving', wrote A Member of the Aristocracy, 'is one of the most important social observances, as it is the groundwork, or nucleus, in general society of all acquaintanceships.'[2]

The cards, contained in an ivory, gold, or silver case, which sometimes also included a washable sheet of thin ivory for note-taking, could express many different meanings. Ladies would leave their card, with 'to inquire' pencilled on it, at one dark, shuttered house of mourning to show their sympathy for the bereaved; they would leave another at a neighbouring house to express their gratitude for the concert they had attended there on the previous afternoon; they would try to gain admittance to an acquaintance's house, but would accept the servant's routine formula 'Not at home, ma'am' (whether it was true or not) and would leave a card with the corner turned down to show that they had called in person; with some trepidation, they would leave yet another card at the house of some higher-ranking lady, without inquiring whether she was at home which might have involved the risk of being snubbed; and if they were leaving town for a time, they would shower all their friends and acquaintances with cards suitably inscribed p.p.c (*pour prendre congé*) to signify their intentions.

What a wealth of information—and excessive anticipations

and disappointed hopes—could be contained in those little slips of pasteboard, no more than $3\frac{1}{2}$ inches wide and $2\frac{1}{2}$ inches deep (but smaller and thinner for a man's), engraved with the caller's name in copper plate and never in old Gothic script, which could cause such a flutter of excitement in the heart of some surprised, lower-ranking recipient and a desperate dash towards Burke's *Peerage* to investigate the unexpected caller's exact degree of rank and precedence. Victorian ladies brought the tragicomedy of card- and name-dropping to a fine art. It was governed by such strict conventions that mistresses were advised to keep a book or a slate in the hall so that forgetful servants could make a written

Musical entertainments were one of the ways Victorians whiled away their afternoons.

record distinguishing those ladies who had only called from the others who had inquired if the mistress was at home, to prevent the solecism (a favourite Victorian word) of calling later on a higher-ranking lady who had merely left her card. The rules of the game were inflexible: a card for a card, and a call for a call. Only ladies of a higher rank were permitted to call on those they did not know, which was no infringement of the rules, but a coveted compliment. A relationship could be ruptured at any time by failing to return a card or a call. It was a quick, efficient, reliable, and sometimes cruel, way of regulating social relationships.

Meanwhile, other ladies would be waiting impatiently in their own drawing rooms to discover what fruits would fall from the earlier dissemination of their cards. In grander houses, and on special occasions, there could sometimes be elaborate afternoon entertainments, with professional singers and accompanists, private dances, or even masked balls. These events were often staged by the *nouveaux riches* in the hope of making new friends and influencing people of a higher social status. The classic method, at all levels of society, was to persuade some high-ranking lady to invite her own wider circle of acquaintances by sending out invitations to the event in her name. In some small country town, a socially ambitious lady might try to induce a local notable to patronise her little afternoon gathering of amateur musicians, just as George Hudson, the 'railway king', who made a fortune in the 1840s by speculation in that new form of transport, persuaded 'several ladies of fashion', including Lady Parkes, to invite the guests to a professional concert in his own home, with such great success that it was attended by 'all the world', including the Duke of Wellington.[3]

Middle-class 'at homes', however, were usually far more modest affairs, where a clutch of local ladies and fewer gentlemen, came in for a quarter of an hour or so between the hours of three and six. The briefness of the visits did not mar the occasion, for success was measured, not by the ticking of a clock, but by significant attendances and absences. It was partly for this grand event that the housemaids had spent the whole morning scrubbing and polishing, dusting and cleaning, and that the parlourmaid had been previously instructed in the niceties of well-born etiquette. For, whatever their private thoughts might be, visitors would judge the event mainly by outer appearances—the cleanliness of the house, the servants' bearing, the mistress's command of small talk—attitudes which did have some justification as these 'at homes' had, after all, very little inner significance.

All servants, even the very highest, the house steward, had some domestic tasks to perform, but the frequency diminished as the pinnacles of the servant hierarchy were reached, where formal or administrative functions gained priority. The housemaids were like stage hands, who set the scenery to create an often false illusion of grandeur; but the parlourmaid had a walk-on part, with a few routine lines, so that her appearance and delivery could help to make or mar the whole social drama. How mortified a mistress would have been if the parlourmaid had kept visitors waiting on the doorstep for five minutes, opening the door after this inexcusable delay, bleary-eyed and slovenly, with a smutty face and bare arms.

Let us spare Victorian ladies their blushes! When the bell rang a neat, pleasant-looking parlourmaid in a clean cap and apron, would open the door immediately and lead the visitor towards the drawing room, where she would pause only to inquire 'What name, please, ma'am?' before she opened the door without knocking. (It was considered extremely vulgar to knock at drawing room doors.) She would be sufficiently discerning to know that two friends should be announced as 'Mrs Smith and

89

van Houten's Cocoa

"THE LATE VISITOR."

No hostess need feel at a disadvantage because of a late visitor if she is using "Van Houten's Cocoa." It is so easily and rapidly made ready, that it provides in a very few moments a refreshing, healthful, and invigorating beverage, absolutely unequalled for its delicious natural flavor.

van Houten's Cocoa

PRE-EMINENT FOR

HIGH QUALITY, DELICIOUS FLAVOR
& ECONOMY IN USE.

VAN HOUTEN'S—THE PREMIER COCOA.

Miss Brown', and that 'Mrs Smith, Miss Brown', was the correct form for two ladies who had happened to arrive together on the doorstep fortuitously. Neither would she offer to take a gentleman's hat, knowing that it would be ill-bred of him not to carry it into the drawing room, where he would deposit it on some convenient chair or table only after he had shaken hands with the hostess.

The parlourmaid brought in afternoon tea between 4 p.m. and 5 p.m., another event with its own elaborate stage management and expensive props: a hanging silver kettle on a stand; silver teapot, cream jug and sugar basin; and dainty cups

Tea is served in the afternoon but the parlourmaid is still expected to be on duty late at night to serve cocoa.

and saucers of rare porcelain. The tea consisted of thin slices of bread and butter, white and brown, and small cakes, such as macaroons, which could be nibbled neatly, as neither plates nor serviettes were provided. Tea cosies were also prohibited as they would have been 'an unconscious confession of impecuniosity or penuriousness'; if the tea was cold it was 'more polite—and the correct thing' to ring the bell and order a fresh supply for the new arrivals.[4] The mistress only poured out the tea and, naturally, never made it, a feat, strange as it may seem, which would have been far beyond her domestic capabilities. When Henrietta

A model layout for the tea-time table with floral decorations.

Litchfield, a daughter of Charles Darwin, was in her eighty-sixth year, she revealed that she had never made a single pot of tea in her whole life.[5] It was a confession which could have been made by many other Victorian ladies.

When a guest was ready to depart, the mistress would ring the bell so that the parlourmaid could be waiting in the front hall to see her out. Mistresses were advised, rather unhelpfully, 'to accompany guests as far towards the door as the circumstances of your friendship seem to demand.'[6]

Elsewhere on the domestic front, everything was, hopefully, quiet with the housemaids studiously mending clothes and linen; the nurse, having returned from her second outing of the day at 4 p.m., washing and tidying up her young charges for their daily encounter with their own mother; and the cook, down in her

deep kitchen, bestirring herself as the hour of five approached, when she would start the main task of the whole day, the cooking of a dinner which consisted of at least five courses.

Mourning, alone, which was not uncommon with the high mortality rate, could enshroud the household in an even deeper afternoon silence and gloom. In aristocratic houses, the funeral hatchment, a diamond-shaped tablet with armorial bearings, was affixed to an outside wall and in more humble homes the shutters were closed and the blinds were drawn. Men put black crêpe bands round their hats and their arms; women wore veils and black dresses covered with crêpe; and both availed themselves of the ever-ready supplies of black-bordered notepaper and handkerchiefs. Mourners were expected to exclude themselves from all society for a fortnight for an uncle or an aunt; two months for a brother or a sister; three to six months for a parent or a child; and a whole year, or even longer, for a husband or a wife. Servants were put into mourning only if the master of the household died, though in that case, they often had something of their own to mourn, as the diminution in the family's income often meant that some, or all, of them lost their jobs.

Dinner is Served!

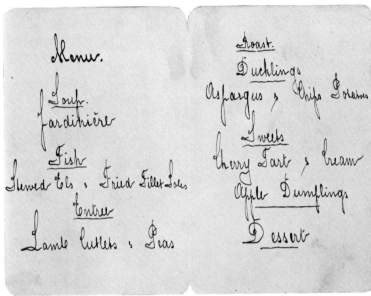

Hand-written menu for a private dinner party in 1891.

Half an hour before dinner, the sound of the gong would rumble through the house, warning members of the family and any house guests to prepare themselves for the culminating event of the social day. The housemaids had already placed jugs of hot water in each bedroom, and stoked up the fires if it was cold; the lady's maid, or the servant who was currently acting in that part, had put out all the clothes and jewels that her mistress would require, or was sometimes already adjusting her steel-hooped crinoline or vigorously brushing and combing her hair. Ladies and gentlemen always wore formal clothes for dinner even if it was only an everyday affair of five courses: soup, fish, meat, sweet or savoury, and dessert. For dinner parties, which were usually held in middle-class homes at least once a month and in some households far more frequently, ladies and gentlemen took even greater care with their appearance.

Dinner parties, which now mean for some English people no more than a couple of bottles of cheap wine and a home-made copy of some exotic dish recollected from a package tour, were far more lavish events in Victorian times, when, in the 1850s,

Hedges and Butler, of Regent Street, London, were retailing champagne at twenty-five shillings a dozen bottles and a choice old cognac cost £3 for twelve bottles at the same merchant's. Although fewer iced lobster soufflés, stuffed quail, and truffles poached in champagne, may have been served in middle-class homes than in the houses of the nobility, the middle classes appear to have fared rather well at their dinner parties if we study the recommended menus of Mrs Beeton, the German-educated author of the classic household work, or, indeed, any other of the cookery books for the middle classes which multiplied in Victorian times.

One actual menu (in French of course) for a dinner party given in a £1,000-a-year middle-class home at the turn of the century, read:

> Consommé Printanier
> Filets de Sole Savoy
> Ris de Veau aux Tomates
> Targets d'Agneau
> Canard sauvage rôti
> Salade verte
> Pudding de Noël
> Paniers d'Orange.
> Laitance de hareng à la diable[1]

The ability to prepare such gastronomic delights made a genuine professed cook the highest-paid and the most independent of all female servants, and even a former head kitchenmaid trained in a noble household was a treasure beyond all price. Unfortunately, these blessings were not easily to be found.

An aroma of mystery still arises from Victorian kitchens. We can read hundreds, no thousands, of mouth-watering menus, but we seek, usually in vain, for much praise of the meals themselves. It is generally acknowledged that the ingredients were superb, though there were some exceptions: French chickens were certainly of superior quality, and some of the fruits and vegetables were allowed to put on weight until they lost all taste and tenderness. Rosa Lewis, the premier dinner-party caterer to the aristocracy in the 1880s, said: 'The gardener in England will grow the gooseberry till it is as big as your head, and the cabbage so large you can't eat it.'[2] But native fruits such as apples and pears, and others grown under glass, such as melons, grapes and pineapples, were as good as any in the whole world, while the home-produced meat from improved strains of fine cattle and lambs, raised on aristocratic pastures, was superb. The high nobility could afford to employ the foremost French and Italian cooks to match the ingredients, so that 'it is allowed by competent judges that a first-rate dinner in England is out of all comparison better than a dinner of the same class·in any other country, for we get the best cooks, as we get the best singers and dancers, by bidding highest for them.'[3]

But even many aristocrats had little appreciation of fine food.

It is well known how one French cook was so deeply wounded by the Duke of Wellington's indifference to his culinary master-pieces that he was forced to hand in his notice. 'I serve him a dinner', said Felix, 'that would make Ude or Francatelli burst with envy, and he says nothing; I serve him a dinner dressed, and badly dressed by the cookmaid, and he says nothing. I cannot live with such a master, if he was a hundred times a hero.'[4] A similar lack of interest was observed among the Cecils later by Viscountess Milner, who had married Lord Edward Cecil, fourth son of the Marquis of Salisbury, in 1894. Dinner, of six or seven courses, was always served by liveried footmen in the great

A dinner party, 1890.

marble hall of Hatfield House, the family seat in Hertfordshire, but 'the Cecils thought very little about what they ate or drank and nothing at all about how it was presented to them', though she conceded that Lord Salisbury had a fine palate for wine.[5]

In truth, many Victorians, including some aristocrats, did not really like foreign 'messed up' food, but preferred traditional fare—sirloins, steaks, hams, pies and puddings—so that meals of this kind continued to be served in less pretentious homes and even in some of the more fashionable when they were dining *en famille*. The unique contribution of the English to gastronomy lay in plain cooking and the making of pies, puddings and tarts (in which they still excel); the kind of meal recommended as fit for an emperor by the Earl of Dudley, who died in 1833, consisting of a good soup, a small turbot, a neck of venison, ducklings with green peas or chicken with asparagus, and an apricot tart. As Abraham Hayward commented ambiguously in 1852: 'Such a dinner can be better served in England than in any other—or, more correctly speaking, there is no other country in the world where it could be served at all.'[6]

Many of the middle classes, at least, also lacked much of a palate for wine, so that they could be easily deceived by unscrupulous German merchants into buying bottles of the favourite aristocratic tipple of sherry and port which had been no nearer to Cadiz or Oporto than Hamburg. One Victorian doctor wrote: 'Hamburg port, which is in fact the "crusty" article that adorns the grocers' windows, consists merely of Elbe water, mixed with a very little light wine of the cheapest kind, strengthened and "fortified" up to the English standard of potency with potato spirit, and flavoured with various ethers to give "bouquet", and coloured with elder wine to afford the rich ruby tint. . . . Elbe sherry is made in just the same manner, with the difference that burnt sugar gives the necessary tint to convert it into an "excellent brown sherry".'[7]

The middle classes were never able to find a sufficient number of good cooks to fulfil their aspirations to a gastronomy which they did not really understand themselves. One of the most frequently quoted maxims among the small minority of Victorian gastronomes was, 'God sends the meat, and the Devil sends the cooks.' In spite of Eliza Acton, Mrs Beeton and many others, there was a lack of skill and devotion among many cooks and an equal lack of knowledge and appreciation among the diners. 'In a vast number of English kitchens', wrote Eliza Acton, 'the cookery fails from the hurried manner in which it is conducted, and from the excess of heat produced by the enormous coal fires kept constantly burning there at all seasons.'[8] She recommended much less fierce roasting and far more slow cooking in the Continental fashion. 'The French people', said Rosa Lewis, 'cook as seriously as they read the Bible.'[9] In England, the priorities were reversed.

Most middle-class ladies had to rely on cooks who professed skills more often than they possessed them. According to the

A model 'space-saving' kitchen of Victorian times.

Servants' Magazine, which should have known, there were far too many cooks with dirty hands and straggling hair, who sometimes had the 'vulgar, disagreeable' habit of taking snuff or scratching their heads, which could be guaranteed to add an unexpected savour to the sauce or the soup. Vegetables and gravy could also acquire a pungent taste if cooks allowed soot to drop into a saucepan or cinders to fall into a dripping tray, as many of them apparently did; while others cooked fish in frying pans which were so greasy that they had accumulated 'a mass of dirt and filth'. The failure to clean all copper saucepans and stewpans thoroughly had far more unpleasant, and sometimes fatal, consequences, as the pans became coated inside with the lethal green rust of verdigris.[10]

Lack of punctuality and foresight were also common failings among cooks, so that the obligatory half-an-hour's chatter in the drawing room before a dinner party, could leave the hostess exhausted with terrifying anticipations of disaster, particularly as rigid conventions prevented her from descending to the kitchen to discover if dinner would be served on time for once. Even when the meal had started, her anxieties were often no less; her fixed smile concealed a dread that cook might have forgotten some essential ingredient for some later course or have burnt the *pièce de résistance*. Even worse tragedies befell some unhappy hostesses. Overheated kitchens gave some cooks an inordinate thirst, and the liberal use of wine and liqueurs in cooking the means to assuage it. Visions of cook being found drunk and incapable cast a long shadow over the anticipated delights of many dinner parties. One high-ranking Army officer became so incensed when he heard that his civilian cook was drunk in the middle of a dinner party that, quite illegally, he called in the military police who carried her 'forcibly downstairs scream-ing'.[11]   Another grievous disturbance to a lady's social

A thumb-print on the plate!

99

engagements could occur if cook were so selfish and inconsiderate to leave suddenly on the morning of a dinner party, just to see her dying mother. The legal right of a mistress to dismiss a servant instantly in such circumstances was upheld in the case of Turner *v* Mason in 1845.[12]

Day-by-day relations between many mistresses and cooks were soured by the latter's claim to all the dripping, or 'kitchen stuff' as it was called, as a perquisite. To increase the size of their golden hoard, some cooks neglected to baste the meat so that even more rich fat and precious juices would run down, hot and sizzling, into their tray; or they cooked with lard or expensive

An example of a Victorian kitchen at Lanhydrock.

butter where dripping would have served. Mistresses suspected, correctly, that dealers who called at kitchen doors to buy the cook's pots of dripping sometimes found concealed slices of meat, lumps of butter or even silver spoons. One Kensington housewife who happened, unusually, to be in her kitchen early one very foggy morning, opened the door when she heard a knock, and had a basin thrust into her hands by a man who said, 'Only three-penn'orth of beef today, and a little gravy'—an experience which should have taught her to keep to her proper station.[13]

Not all mistresses suffered such misfortunes. The majority of cooks were probably honest and did their best, though often that did not amount to much, as there was no real means of training them except, empirically, in the households of the nobility, which was not of much benefit to the middle classes. In 1857, a school of cookery was set up in Mortimer Street, London, to instruct a few children from Christchurch National School, St Pancras, in plain cookery before they went into service; later a class in professed cookery was opened, too.[14] Three years after that, a Mrs Mitchell established another school nearby in Great Portland Street, to teach professed cookery to servants. More schools were opened in London in the 1880s, but there were never enough to make much difference to the general standards of cooking.

In some ways it did not matter, as dinner parties in middle-class homes were far more social than gastronomic events, in which conspicuous expenditure and display were given precedence. In the 1840s Elizabeth Davis found that her employer, an extremely rich heiress, could never resist the challenge of buying whatever food happened to be the most expensive on that day. When she was told the price, she patted her pocket, and said: 'Do you know who I am? Mrs U——, with eight thousand pounds a year pocket money, that no one can touch.'[15]

From the moment dinner-party guests started to arrive, a quarter of an hour before the stipulated time of eight o'clock, they were encaptured in a ritual cage of prescribed behaviour which was as restrictive as the boned stays the ladies wore. On this occasion it was correct for the parlourmaid to take the gentlemen's hats and the ladies' cloaks, though the latter kept their gloves on until they sat down at the dining-room table. The parlourmaid would show them to the drawing room where they might amuse themselves by leafing through those large leather-bound albums of what then seemed miraculous photographs, or by engaging in small, and usually vapid, talk. At 8.15 precisely (unless the cook was otherwise indisposed), the parlourmaid would throw open the drawing-room door (without knocking) and announce in a clear voice, 'Dinner is served.' Without delay, the ladies and gentlemen would rise (if they were not already standing) and file out in a previously-arranged pattern of precedence, led by the host with the lady of the highest rank on his right arm, and with the hostess and the highest-ranking gentleman forming the rearguard.

If the parlourmaid had taken extra care in setting the table, there might even be some little appreciative gasps of praise as the guests entered the dining room. The long table, covered by a spotless white damask cloth, might be lit by a dozen shaded candles in silver candelabra or by one or two handsome lamps, whose soft rose-coloured rays would glitter on the shining silver cutlery, the immaculate glasses, and the centrepiece consisting of the family's most valuable epergne, full of colourful flowers, moss or grasses. There might also be, in uncluttered parts of the table, some small trails of ivy curling around single exotic blooms; porcelain holders containing the hand-written menus; and sometimes a silver bowl of melons, pineapples, peaches, pears and grapes.

In many middle-class homes, diners took their seats at the table in the same order of precedence as they had entered the room; high nobility, who could afford to ignore rank if it was more convenient to do so, more often seated guests in such a way that friction would produce sparkling conversation. Some, like Lord Russell, did not always insist that gentlemen should dress for dinner. But these were aristocratic individualities that most middle-class people would have feared to adopt.

Both the cookery and the service at English dinner parties had been copied from foreign countries. Snob cooking was French, and in some old-fashioned homes, meals were served *à la française*, with a choice of courses being placed on the table at the same time; but, from about the middle of the nineteenth century, *service à la Russe* became more fashionable, with each course being served separately from a sidetable. The latter method needed on average one servant to every three diners, so that the middle classes commonly adopted a compromise, in which the host served the soup, fish, meat and game or poultry; the hostess served the tarts, sweets and dessert; while the parlourmaid brought the dishes in from the kitchen and handed round the vegetables and the side dishes.

While they were eating, ladies and gentlemen—if they did not want to be considered of low breeding—had to mind their P's and Q's, remembering that peas themselves always had to be eaten with a fork, which was also used for jellies, blancmanges and iced puddings. (In eating a tart, it was permissible to eat the fruit and the juice with a spoon, but the pastry had to be eaten with a fork.) To put a knife into one's mouth at any time was a grave social offence if one were British, though it was accepted that foreigners (who, obviously, could not be expected to know any better), even those of 'high rank and unquestionable breeding', could indulge in 'great feats of knife-swallowing' at meals.[16] To pick up a chicken bone was even more unpardonable; though some aristocratic ladies (English ones, too) had enough common sense to gnaw a tasty bone at their dinner parties.

Ten minutes or so after the dessert had been eaten and the finger bowls used (not for gargling, Mrs Beeton warned), the hostess would bow knowingly to the highest-ranking lady, and all the ladies would rise, draw on their gloves, fling their table napkins carelessly on the chair (for the parlourmaid to pick up later), and withdraw in order of precedence again to the drawing room, where coffee would be served. Meanwhile, the gentlemen would close ranks at the table and circulate a bottle of vintage claret or crusted port before they also left the room to join the

Gentlemen enjoying after-dinner drinks.

ladies. The host was advised to suggest an adjournment when he observed 'a general indication of restlessness on the part of his guests, and an apparent wish to do so, by their looking at their watches and yawning', which was scarcely a tribute to the average Victorian gentleman's powers of diversion.[17]

By 10:30, or even earlier, the ordeal was over. Speed and efficiency gradually came to dominate in all middle-class social engagements; in aristocratic circles, on the other hand, the most entertaining and interesting time came after the dinner was over when the really prominent people often dropped in for a chat. Middle-class men gradually reduced the length of time they spent over their port or claret from an hour to fifteen or twenty minutes. The feeding time was also shortened. 'No dinner', Lady Jeune declared imperiously in 1895, 'should last more than an hour and a quarter if properly served', which was scarcely the attitude of a gastronome indulging in a seven-course meal.[18]

Although the diners might rush through their courses, like horses at a steeplechase, there could be no equivalent shortening

of the time the servants had to spend in preparing them. The servants' weekly workload was actually increased as Sunday night, which had once been quiet, became increasingly popular for dinner parties, with growing anti-Sabbatarianism. To cook the dinner took at least three hours, in addition to the previous hours of preparation. The servants had to snatch their own meagre supper of bread and cheese (or cheese and bread, as they might have said) when they could, as they still had many tasks to perform that evening. Unless she was intoxicated again, cook could not be really happy until the final course was successfully served, which would release her from her three-hour vigil over the range, which was roaring like a furnace. The parlourmaid, who might have started work at seven in the morning, still had to drag herself, pale-faced and aching, round the dining room, to serve the coffee, to clear the table, and still be ready, wanly smiling, to show the visitors to the door when they left. The housemaids had to tidy the bedrooms, to take the dirty shoes and boots downstairs to be cleaned, to turn down the sheets on the bed, to put a warming pan or a hot-water bottle in each bed, to get the baths ready for the morning, and, finally, just before the family and any houseguests retired, to put cans of hot water in each bedroom. The lady's maid had to wait up until her mistress chose to go to bed (whatever the hour), so that she could release her from her imprisoning stays and put away her clothes and jewellery.

Then there was the washing up. Someone had to do it that night, whether it was the parlourmaid, the housemaid, the cook, or all of them together. Even a small dinner party for eight could produce well over fifty dirty knives and forks, about thirty spoons, the same number of glasses, and a hundred or more plates and dishes, in addition to all the kitchen equipment and cooking utensils: stewpans and sauté pans of various materials and sizes; frying pans; steamers; spring jacks; and bottle-jacks, enclosed in a dome-shaped cover, which cooked by radiant heat. Washing up was not a sinecure. One butler's recommended method was: put warm water and soda in sink or tub and wash glasses; put in soft soap, add more water; put away glasses after polishing; whisk water into lather; put small silver to soak; prepare plates by scraping; wash small silver and rinse in very hot water, and wipe while still hot; add hot water, and more soda, and soak plates; pack small silver and put away; wash plates and rinse in hot water; hold knives in hot water for a few seconds and brush separately; wash cups and saucers singly to prevent chipping.[19]

When all of these duties had been performed, the servants were at liberty to go to bed, unless there were any further late-night requests, and to sleep, happily, we hope, until they got up with the lark again the next morning. And so it went on day after day after day. . . .

Home baking in the kitchen of a country house, 1850.

Maids-of-all-Work and Charity

For young, inexperienced recruits, the biggest disadvantage in domestic service often proved to be the very one they had least expected: the isolation and the loneliness of their lives. We, too, who have been raised on television serials of high life below stairs, now often share their misapprehensions, for downstairs drama and romance were confined mainly to the houses of the nobility and of the upper middle classes, where large staffs of servants were employed. Servants who worked with other servants were in a minority. In mid-Victorian times, about six out of every ten female servants worked alone as general maids, who were expected to perform all the formal duties and chores (apart from the laundry which was invariably sent out), with only the occasional assistance of a charwoman or the casual help of a little ten-or eleven-year-old 'step girl', who would whiten the front door step and clean the windows for a copper or two. Like some quick-change *artiste* in a fourth-rate palace of varieties, general servants were expected to play the part of housemaid, nurse, parlourmaid and cook as the need arose, without any aid from the daughters of the house (who were too busily engaged in piano-playing, cross-stitch or crochet) and not much more help from the mistress. Their brief contacts with the world outside were restricted mainly to visits by tradesmen, who called at the side or the back door, and by 'ladies' and 'gentlemen' who rang at the front. Their nights were short, lonely intermissions between the burdens of one day and the next; their days were measured out in square yards of floor space. One little maid-of-all-work from South Hackney, a former battered baby whose right arm had been wrenched out of its socket by her drunken mother, was taken to the National Gallery one day by a 'lady journalist'; but she did not even glance at the paintings and only said: 'My, how these 'ere floors must make some one's arms ache. It would kill me to scrub 'em entirely.'[1]

Conditions in one-servant households included both the best and the very worst. In the villages of England, there were still many homes where the single servant, in the words of one official report of 1899, 'can secure for herself such warm appreciation from the family she serves, that her privileges and freedom quite outweigh the attractions of better paid service in richer households'.[2] But there were many other households, especially

Maid-of-all-work at a Watford public
house, 1862.

in the cities, where the only servant employed was not an integrated member of the household and the local community, but a twelve- or thirteen-year-old maid-of-all-work from some distant place. These 'slaveys', who were also known as 'trotters' or 'strikers', often had to work from 5 a.m. to midnight for a wage of £6 or £7 *a year*. The American writer, J Fenimore Cooper, was appalled by the brutal way in which they were treated. 'These poor creatures', he wrote, 'have an air of dogged sullen misery that I have never seen equalled in any other class of human being, not even excepting the beggars in the streets.' He remembered one little 'slavey' who came into his room at 'a sort of drilled trot, as if she had been taught a particular movement to denote assiduity and diligence, and she never presumed to raise her eyes to mine, but stood the whole time looking meekly down.'[3] On the whole, the nearer the maid and the mistress were in social class, the worse the maid was treated; for the mistress needed to prove her own superiority and to ensure her own personal progress by exploiting the maid as much as possible.

Let us listen to one eighteen-year-old girl who had worked as a 'slavey' from the age of thirteen to fifteen.

Oh, I've been a servant for years! I learnt ironing off the lady; I didn't know nothing about it. I didn't know nothing about anything. I didn't know where to buy the wood for the fire. I run along the street and asked the first person I sor where the wood-shop was.

I was frightened—oh, I was. They wasn't particular kind in my first place. I had plenty to eat—it wasn't anything of that. They jest give me an egg and says, 'There, get your dinner', but not anything more.

I had to do all the work. I'd no one to go to. Oh! I cried the first night. I used to cry so.

I had always slep in a ward full of other girls, and there I was alone, and this was a great big house—oh, so big! and they told me to go downstairs, in a room by the kitchen all alone, with a long black passage. I might have screamed, but nobody would have heard. An archytec, the gen'lman was. . . .

Then I got a place in a family where there was nine children. I was about fourteen then. I earned two shillings a week.

I used to get up and light the fire, bath them and dress them, and git their breakfast, and the lady sometimes would go up to London on business, and then I had the baby too, and it couldn't be left, and had to be fed.

I'd take them all out for a day's walk on the common. There was one a cripple. She couldn't walk about. She was about nine year old. I used to carry her on my back.

Then there was dinner, and to wash up after; and then by that time it would be tea-time agin. And then I had to put the nine children to bed and bath them, and clean up the rooms and the fires at night; there was no time in the morning. And then there would be the gen'lman's supper to get.

Oh! that was a hard place. I wasn't in bed till twelve, and I'd be up by six. I stopped there nine months. I hadn't no one to help me. Oh, yes, I had: the baker, he told me of another place.

Hannah Cullwick scrubbing the
doorstep of her mistress's house
c. 1872. She secretly married the
wealthy lawyer, Arthur Munby, who
became a champion of the servant
cause. Munby took this photograph
and the one on p. 107.

I've been here three year. I'm cook, and they are very kind; but I tell the girls there's none on 'em had such work as me.[4]

This girl was recruited, like many other maids-of-all-work, from the workhouse, which has always been scoured throughout English history whenever there was a demand for cheap labour—at sea, in the early cotton mills, for road-making, or on the domestic front. In 1850, most girls of twelve or thirteen had already been despatched from all the workhouses in Shropshire for domestic service; but very few liked the life and soon left to work on farms instead.[5] Twenty years later a new national scheme made it possible for approved families to take workhouse girls into their homes as foster children who would, allegedly, be trained for service: the more alert members of the middle classes were quick to seize this golden chance to employ subsidised domestic labour. Many of the girls were sent to distant homes. The workhouse at Windermere, Westmorland, for instance, sent children to a school inspector in Derby, a professor in Durham and a tradesman in Manchester.[6]

The employment of workhouse girls as domestic servants appears to have brought few benefits to mistresses or maids. The only thorough investigation into the subject, carried out in London between 1871 and 1872, showed that only 16 per cent of the girls were given good marks by their mistresses; 30 per cent were considered 'fair'; 38 per cent were rated 'unsatisfactory'; and 16 per cent were described as 'bad'. Although the workhouses claimed that the children were already trained for service, many mistresses found that, in addition to their other manifold faults, they were often totally lacking in domestic abilities. One 'unsatisfactory' girl was described by her mistress as 'a pilferer; untruthful, idle; incorrigibly dirty in habits. Can scrub a floor, but has no other accomplishments.' A comment on another child read: 'Girl said she had never lit a fire or cleaned a grate, but as she never spoke the truth about anything, probably she lied there.' A number were unsound in both body and in mind: one 'half-witted' orphan was round-backed and un-healthy, with one eye permanently dimmed by disease. No less than 8 per cent of the girls had weak or seriously defective eyesight. Another girl, who was described as 'strong in body, but deficient in mind', was told to sweep the bedroom. When her mistress returned, expecting to find the room neat and tidy, she found to her amazement and annoyance that the girl had trodden all the tea leaves firmly into the carpet.

Lacking the security of a family, friends and home, these girls often reacted violently to any real imposition or imagined slight. One not unintelligent fifteen-year-old girl, whose father was dead and whose mother was still living in a workhouse, would 'sing like a bird' at her work when she was in a good mood. But 'when she took a fit of sulks, nothing could be done with her. She would fold her arms and stand behind the kitchen door, and absolutely refuse to do anything.' Others howled and screamed in their rage until a crowd gathered threateningly outside the house to the alarm of the mistress. Mistresses, who tested the girls' honesty by leaving a coin under the carpet (a common stratagem in many Victorian homes), often had their worst expectations confirmed. Some of the girls were violent. One threatened to stab the nurse; another broke a plate over the head of a fellow servant. About 8 per cent absconded and another $2\frac{1}{2}$ per cent were known, or believed, to have 'fallen', joining the many other former servants who had sunk into the vast underworld of vice and crime in the capital. One girl, who left service to marry a £2-a-week house painter, soon discovered that

Many young girls must have been happy to escape from the workhouse which was often the only alternative to a life in service. This photograph was taken at St Pancras workhouse at the turn of the century.

he was nothing but a pimp; another girl, who was dismissed for theft and violence, was later seen by the daughter of the house, walking along the street 'with long curls down her back, and not looking respectable.'[7] It was amazing what some mistresses, obviously not uneducated, would put up with, just in the hope of getting cheap domestic labour.

Although genuine concern for these deprived children did exist in individual cases, there was no more general solicitude than there had been earlier when pauper boys and girls had been sent off by the wagon-load, literally, to the early cotton mills—perhaps even less as the latter's conditions of work had, at least, been controlled eventually by Acts of Parliament. It was often claimed—and still is—that it would have been impossible to make laws to protect domestic servants and, certainly, they would have been difficult to administer; but it is curious how practically all of the domestic law that did exist was weighted heavily in the favour of the master and the mistress, so that if anyone suffered it should not be them. If a servant was dismissed and her wages or her box were withheld illegally by the mistress, a magistrate had no legal right to interfere. A few sympathetic magistrates, like Mr C K Murray, of Union Hall Police Court, London, would sometimes grant a summons for the employer to show cause why the box had been detained; but if the employer refused to attend a hearing, there was no further action he could take.[8] Servants could sue their employers in the civil court for the return of their box; but, even if they had been able to raise

The cook appeals in vain against her dismissal.

the money to do so, they would probably never have been able to obtain another job. Mr Murray's pleas for the law to be amended in the servants' favour were ignored.

Servants were liable to instant dismissal if they disobeyed any legal, though totally unreasonable order. Employers were not bound (though many did) to provide medical care for a servant, even though the cause of their illness might lie in their own home. Neither were employers legally obliged to provide a servant with a character, or reference, which gave the mistress the whiphand in all disputes, as a girl without a character would find it virtually impossible to get another situation. (Although German servants were often lower paid and harder worked, they had by law to be given a written reference in their contract of employment book, which was safeguarded with typical Teutonic thoroughness in the local police station.)

Servants of all classes had very few rights, and not many prospects for the future, apart from the fortunate minority who worked in some big houses or in the home of a benevolent employer. The young 'slavey', working in a lodging house or a coffee shop or with 'rough-mannered' employers had to 'work harder and under more unfavourable conditions perhaps than any other class of the community. . . . As soon as she reaches an age when she wants more than a very small sum in wages, she is dismissed and replaced by another young girl. . . . This class of girl in a very few years disappears from the ranks of domestic servants, and in doing so, is generally in a worse position than the factory girl in the same grade.'[9] But many mature women, who had devoted years of service to the same family, sometimes renouncing marriage and always much of her personal life to do so, could in the end often look forward to little more than the maid-of-all-work. There might be a few words of thanks, a month's wages, and a small token of esteem from some charity, such as the Female Servants' Home Society, which gave a Bible for two years' continuous service; a testimonial and a suitable book for five; a silver medal for nine; and a gold medal for fifteen.[10] Apart from these doles from charities, or the more unlikely chance of a large bequest from some grateful employer, there was nothing awaiting many servants in old age or illness than the almshouse or the workhouse, as even a casual glance at any workhouse register will show. 'Service is no inheritance' was a maxim often on the lips of Victorian servants and even more frequently in their minds.

Charities, some of great antiquity, provided little gifts of goods or money to selected servants in many different parts of the country, often on St Thomas's Day, which falls four days before Christmas. James Frethern's Charity, for instance, was founded in 1663 'for the benefit of a maid servant who has continued six years as a hired servant in Burford, Oxfordshire'; the Rev. Walter Sellon's Charity at Wargrave, Berkshire, was established in 1793 to provide eight guineas 'for the benefit of poor persons resident in the parish who are engaged in domestic service'; and the Margaret Dew Charity, of 1816, was for the 'general benefit of Godly and deserving poor and decayed Housekeepers of Bramton Abbots parish', Hertfordshire.[11] These servant charities, and many more, are on the active register of the Charity Commission to this very day, even though there is now, fortunately, little call on their assistance; but in Victorian times it was different. On December 23, 1869, Lady Knightley of Fawsley, Northamptonshire, spent a happy evening in the servants' hall watching her husband—'dear Rainald'—distribute gifts to the inhabitants of six surrounding villages. She commented: 'The system is admirable, and has gone on for

Charming Lady: (showing her house to benevolent old gentleman) 'That's where the housemaid sleeps.'
Benevolent old gentleman: 'Dear me, you don't say so! Isn't it very damp? I see the water glistening on the walls.'
Charming Lady: 'Oh, it's not too damp for a servant.'

generations, and it was pleasant to see the poor women trotting off with their bundles of calico, flannel and blankets.'[12]

Although it might not have been so pleasant for these women to walk many miles back home along muddy lanes on a freezing night, clutching their small bundles, they were used to it, like all country folk; these gifts were so important to them, that their distribution sometimes aroused bitter controversy, with appeals from the decisions of trustees being made to the majestic authority of the Charity Commissioners. This happened in the case of Ellen Martin, a servant at the Old George Tavern in Stanhope Street, the Strand, London, who had been refused a gift from a charity because she worked in a public house. The landlady's husband then wrote to the commissioners to defend the claims of his servant and the honour of his outraged wife:

Mrs Jupp (late Mrs Binstead) has been the landlady of the above tavern for 35 years, during which period there has not been a single complaint against the management; so I think I am justified in saying that the house is respectably conducted. She has always subscribed to all the institutions connected with the parish of Clement Danes—such as Hospitals, Dispensary Schools etc., which I also do at present.

There is a Gift in the parish, the 'Isaac Duckett Charity' for domestic servants who are 25 years of age, and have been in one situation in the parish for 7 years.

A servant of ours (Ellen Martin) who has been with us since April 1880—and is with us now—7 years as domestic servant and 2½ years as domestic servant and barmaid combined (a most respectable young woman) applied on the 24th July for the parish gift, and was told, to my great surprise, she was not qualified.

But the Commissioners found that the trustees had acted in accordance with the terms of the bequest and upheld their decision.[13] (There was another storm in a teacup over the St Andrew's branch of the same charity some thirty-five years later, when two maids working for a solicitor and three maids at St Andrew's Rectory, were also refused a gift, because of a boundary change by Act of Parliament.)[14]

Servants' charities and institutions of all kinds were severely handicapped by a chronic shortage of funds in Victorian times. Mistresses were reluctant to give servants money either in the form of well-earned wages or in charitable donations. In 1861, only £6,250 was subscribed to the twenty-one servant charities in the capital; Bible and missionary societies, on the other hand, received no less than £332,679.[15] The Victorians had an inflexible, and often unfeeling, sense of priorities.

Servants were sometimes deprived of much bigger benefits than the Isaac Duckett gift of £5 to £20 through legal technicalities. One Victorian servant, Elizabeth Davis, the housekeeper to a London lawyer, had hoped to become a rich woman with an income of £4,000 a year when her employer died; but her dreams of wealth were shattered when her master's will was successfully disputed because it had not been correctly witnessed. Instead of inheriting an estate in Wiltshire, several farms and houses, she got nothing 'but a few old things, which I afterwards sold for fifteen shillings'.[16] Later, she went out to the Crimea with Florence Nightingale as a nurse.

Another Victorian housekeeper, Nancy Goodall, was somewhat luckier. Just before he died, her employer had added a codicil to his will, leaving Nancy a 'comfortable provision' for the rest of her life; but his will was disputed by relatives on the ground of his alleged insanity. After thirty years' faithful service, poor Nancy was thrown out of the London house in Piccadilly at the age of fifty, with nothing but a quarter's wages in her pocket. An even greater disaster followed. While she was searching for lodgings, she was knocked down by a coach and, as a result, became a cripple for life. But in this case there was a happy ending. With her indomitable 'pride' and courage, she started work as a clogmaker, which she could do sitting down, and later, when the case had eventually been settled in the Court of Chancery, she got her annuity and retired happily to her native village.[17]

For those servants who received no bequest or no help from a charity the main alternative in old age or in times of illness or misfortune was the workhouse. Behind the bare formal records of name, occupation, date of birth, religion, date of admission and discharge, it is possible to discern in any workhouse register many different stories of heart-breaking tragedy and inability to cope with life. In 1869 the regular patrons of the Union Workhouse in Winchester, Hampshire, included the four Bunce women—Elizabeth, Maria, Emily Kate and Pressila [sic]—who obviously used the workhouse as a hostel, either singly or together, whenever they felt in need of a change or a rest. There were other older servants, like 48-year-old Mary Ann Baker, a notorious character, who shuttled back and forth between workhouse and situation, never staying long in either, as she was prone to use 'very bad language and cause disturbance in every part of the workhouse'. There was also a younger version, Ann Sims, who was already at the age of twenty reacting violently against her lot in life: she came in for a single day in June; returned for three days in September; and reappeared again in October when she was given into custody for breaking workhouse windows.

Many servants, appalled perhaps by the harsh conditions, couldn't bear to stay there for more than a couple of days: Ann Bussen, aged seventeen, was admitted before supper on Monday and discharged herself before breakfast on Wednesday; while Sarah Neil, a 36-year-old charwoman, stayed only from Thursday to Saturday, leaving, as she had arrived, with her four-year-old son Thomas and her year-old baby, Julia. Other servants stayed longer, like poor Georgina Taylor, aged twenty-three, who was admitted on Saturday, May 8 and discharged on her own order on Tuesday, August 3, with a little baby girl, described as 'good' by officials of the workhouse where it had been born. Others, like 22-year-old Jane Batchelor, a member of the Society of Christians, came in with her new-born babe for a month and left again we do not know for where.[18] And so the sorry tale continues down the years, as these servants shifted fecklessly from situation to the workhouse and back again, leaving these unfinished records as almost the only sole memorial of their unavailing and burdensome lives.

Fallen Women

The majority of female servants were honest, moral and respectable, retaining their 'honour' (as Victorian ladies would have said) until they married. Like other young women in ages past, they yearned for love and marriage, foolishly, perhaps, before they entered their first situation, with the handsome son of a rich employer, though such false hopes usually led only to their seduction. Later, as reality intervened, and their life in service became increasingly distasteful, or even repugnant, they lowered their sights to some man who was more immediately attainable.

Their choice of marriage partner was usually severely restricted by their class and their situation. Some governesses were enabled to regain through marriage the status of which they had been deprived by their father's misfortune or mismanagement; and a few servants, especially in the eighteenth century, made even more advantageous alliances. In 1763, Thomas Coutts, co-founder of the bank that bears his name, married his brother's housemaid, Susannah Starkie, the daughter of a small farmer from Lancashire. Before she died in 1815, she had seen her first daughter marry the third Earl of Guilford; her second daughter, the first Marquis of Bute; and her third, Sir Francis Burdett. (Her husband's fortune was, of course, the big attraction.) Samuel Horsley, Bishop of St Asaph, also married a servant. Shortly after his first wife died in 1777, he married her maid, Sarah Wright. Edward Miles, a nineteenth-century Quaker, not only had two careers as a druggist and a dentist but also two wives—the second under common law—both of whom were servants.[1]

Such marriages were commonplace in 'silly, sensational' magazines, but much more exceptional in real life. The peak of most girls' possibilities had been reached, if they were fortunate enough to marry an honest butler or footman, who might then set up as a shopkeeper, a cabbie, a publican or a boarding-house keeper on their joint savings, small businesses which seem to have failed almost as often as they succeeded. Otherwise, they could hope to marry a man of no higher social standing than a groom, a tradesman, a policeman, a soldier, or a sailor. Many of them returned home, with their little nest eggs, to marry the 'penny post correspondent' whom they had left behind in their own village years before.

Unmarried mistresses were always ready to give their maids good advice. The caption read:
Miss Lonely: 'You ought to be careful Kitty. Marriage is a very serious matter.'
The Maid: (who has had a proposal) 'Yes Ma'am; but staying single is a serious matter, too.'

Meanwhile, most had been exposed to many perils and temptations, particularly in those houses which were rich enough to employ male servants and to entertain a constant succession of guests. Many men servants had just as honourable intentions as the girls and women; but employers' dislike of keeping married men on their staffs (particularly in the early part of the century) sometimes diverted their libidinous drives into underground channels. With their large accumulations of unspent wages, male servants were among the readiest purchasers (with some rich employers) of the vast amount of high-priced pornographic literature which circulated in Victorian times.[2] The study of these periodicals and books, however, sometimes served only to increase their real-life appetites, so that there was frequently some opportunistic footman on the staff licking his lips in anticipation of the arrival of the next naïve maid from the countryside. Gentlemen guests could be just as big a menace to honest girls. Rosa Lewis, who started work at the age of twelve as a shilling-a-week scullery maid in the home of the Comte de Paris at Mortlake, remembered how she used to barricade her door against male guests 'thinking that they were going to get me'. One night she went back to her bedroom above the laundry to find a gentleman already waiting there 'in a tight sort of pyjamas', but she had enough sense to scream at the top of her voice and threaten to inform on him, which was enough to send him away with desires unfulfilled. Such simple stratagems, however, were not always effective: Rosa had seen many of her fellow servants leave with their little yellow bags in the morning, for it was the victim who was told to leave, not the seducer.[3]

Employers' sons presented just as big a threat to servant girls, especially those who were so keen to marry above their station that they could convince themselves that the wedding banns had actually been put up in some conveniently remote parish already. This classic method of attempted seduction was employed against one young maid-of-all-work who was working at Epsom, Surrey. The son of the house told the maid that he had put up the banns in a London parish. Shortly afterwards, he took her for a walk one night in a dark and lonely wood; but, at the last minute, overcome apparently by fears of possible consequences, he started talking about a man who had just been

A horrified mistress surprises her husband with a servant-girl in this Cruikshank drawing entitled, 'Check Mate'.

hanged for 'an outrage on a female' and asked if she 'could have the heart to swear a man's life away'. Not surprisingly, at this point, she took to her heels and reached the house in safety, undefiled.[4]

The streets were no safer than some big houses, though many inconsiderate masters and mistresses continued to send young servant girls out on errands at night. In Glasgow, one young 'gentleman' followed a fifteen-year-old maid to a washer-woman's house persistently for a whole month, making all kinds of offers and promises. Finally, he actually followed her into the house, where he met his match, as the washerwoman set about him with her tongs, drove him downstairs, and then escorted the girl safely back to her employer.[5] Victorian streets at night were full of importunate and disreputable gentlemen and many other threats and temptations. Ports were overrun by sailors with full pockets and empty nights, while the streets of London and of other garrison towns were full of uniformed soldiers—a sight which was colourful enough to infect any young saucy servant girl with what was then called the 'scarlet fever'.

Not all servant girls were unwilling partners in venereal adventures. The sexual standards of the countryside, where so many of them had been born, were very different from those of drawing rooms in the towns. Their youthful observation of natural activities in barns and fields had stripped sex of the middle-class sense of shame. The long-established traditions of wife-swopping and trial marriage ('hand-fasting' in Scotland and 'bundling' in Wales) persisted in many rural areas throughout the reign, with other, ancient orgiastic rites; while the annual hiring fairs for farm and domestic servants often ended in drunken debauchery.

It was only natural that some of these girls, thwarted by the almost universal ban on followers, should have found another outlet for their natural instincts. For this reason, many household sons found far more co-operation than they might have expected in their first fumbling experiments with the household maids. One schoolboy wrote to his friend during the holidays: 'I've had fine times with my mother's maid. She's a ripping girl! She helps me to dress, and so on, as my mother won't get a man-servant for me yet, thinking the maid can do all I want. I don't mind a bit, as you may suppose. Mignon brings up a cup of coffee in the morning, and we always have a lark together then. She used to start by tickling my feet, but she soon got more daring, and would pull the clothes off and pinch my legs.' These preliminary 'larks' often culminated in some full-length adventure; but in this case they had to stop short at heavy petting as Mignon already had a 'frightfully jealous' lover.[6]

There was always a minority of servant girls who would prostitute themselves for their 'own pleasure, a few trifling presents or a little money now and then'.[7] These 'dollymops', as they were called, paraded provocatively in public parks; they smiled engagingly from area steps; they haunted dancing rooms,

This servant girl leads a vicarious romantic life by reading her mistress's love letters.

A crude illustration of the Victorian prostitute at work in the Haymarket at midnight. The slight lifting of the skirt-hem constitutes a proposition.

taverns and casinos. There is no means of knowing how many servants were also part-time prostitutes, or enthusiastic amateurs as we might call them, but according to some contemporary experts the number was surprisingly high.

One of the greatest authorities on early Victorian prostitution was William Tait, who saw many of the final, and often fatal, consequences in Edinburgh Lock Hospital (for venereal diseases), where he was the house surgeon. He estimated that there were about eight hundred full-time professionals in the Scottish capital; but, in addition, there were no less than three hundred servants working part-time at the same trade. Nurses, who had the greatest freedom to spend many hours out of doors, were sometimes inclined to combine their regular calling with a little moonlighting, even, occasionally, in broad daylight. One nurse from 'a very respectable family' used to leave her two young children sitting in the High Street, while she went off to oblige a gentleman in a house of assignation nearby. Most of these 'clandestine prostitutes' were 'common servants', like the one from Leith who visited a house in Edinburgh every alternate Sunday night for four years; but governesses, ladies' maids and housekeepers were also involved.

Scene at a 'Nighthouse', a London meeting place for prostitutes and gentlemen.

When the master of the house had similar predilections to his servants some unlikely encounters could result. One gentleman, who was visiting a house of assignation in the New Town, Edinburgh, was astonished to find his own children waiting outside. On making inquiries, he discovered that his nursemaid was already in one of the apartments with a gentleman. Another master who was visiting a similar house was delighted to be told that he would be provided with 'a lady newly arrived from the country'; but to his amazement he was brought face to face, and body to body, with his own housekeeper, though what they said—or did—is not, unfortunately, recorded.[8]

Superintendent James Dunlap, who had been in charge of 'C' Division of the Metropolitan Police since 1868, told one official inquiry in 1881 about part-time prostitution among servants in the then notorious district of St James's:

Dunlap: There are a lot of little servant girls about my division in lodgings, and in other places; they are of every kind; they get small wages; they come out on errands; they see these girls walking about the streets, their equal in social standing; they see them dressed in silk and satins; they do not think of the way they get their money; they say, 'You can go and dress in silks and satins', while I am slaving; they talk to the girls, and they are influenced. . . .

Chairman: In the case of servants, I suppose it is hardly possible that they can follow any life of prostitution, because they would lose their places would they not?

Dunlap: They could not follow what you may call prostitution, but I am afraid many of them are far from virtuous; the term 'prostitute' would not be a proper one to apply to them, but no doubt many of them have intercourse with men.[9]

Most Victorian ladies recoiled with horror from such shameless girls, particularly if they were unfortunate enough to find one on their own premises; but how much greater might their own sense of shame have been if they had acknowledged their own responsibility for driving so many young servant girls into an even more debauched life of full-time prostitution, in which the average expectancy of life was no more than five or six years? Their pitiless dismissals of girls who gave the slightest offence—or none—and their insatiable demands for recruits helped to fill the disreputable registry offices, and ultimately the brothels, of London and other big cities with new victims.

The majority of registry offices were run by honest men and women or by charities. They provided recruits and unemployed servants with spartan, but cheap, accommodation, where girls could share a bed with one, or sometimes, two others, while they waited for a mistress to engage them. But there were fringe offices, recorded in police files and in the 'black book' of the National Vigilance Association, which tricked and deceived both mistresses and maids and acted as the biggest recruitment agencies for the brothels of all categories at the heart of Victorian cities. One London agency, run by a former detective, not only sent many servants into brothels, but also swindled mistresses by keeping a decoy of half a dozen, neatly dressed, good-looking servant girls on the premises who, on one pretext or another, always failed to arrive at their new situation once the naïve mistress had paid the hiring fee. This registry office, which lured girls to its doors by dishonest advertisements of high wages and little work, was closed by the police; but the owner changed his name and almost immediately opened another office.[10]

It was often difficult for the police to accumulate sufficient evidence to bring charges. The owner of one agency in Bishops Road, London, was ultimately convicted of obtaining half a crown by false pretences from an 18-year-old girl who had been induced to leave a good situation in Worcester in the hope of obtaining an even better job as a lady's maid in the capital.[11] Another office in Park Street, London, was closed by the proprietor before any charges could be made, after the police had begun to investigate complaints by girls from many different parts of the country.[12] One London brothel employed a procuress at 'a considerable salary' to go out into the country to hire young girls, often with their parents' consent, for some fictitious situation in the capital: on arrival, they were taken direct to the brothel, where 'their ruin was effected'.[13] One London brothel keeper, a Mrs Harris, set up a fake servants' agency on the Slough–Windsor road and employed her sister, Mrs Barnett, to recruit good-looking local girls for service. After they had been engaged, they were sent first to Mrs Harris's highest-class establishment in Great Titchfield Street, in the heart of London, and then relegated in uneasy stages to the five other lower-class bordellos she owned in the capital.[14]

Some fringe agencies employed procuresses to loiter around

Madame turns the head of an innocent victim by tempting her with finery.

railway stations—'fiends in women's attire', as the *Servants' Magazine* warned its unsuspecting readers—who could trap innocent girls into 'disgrace, disease, and hasty death'.[15] One of their favourite tricks was to enter into conversation with some naïve-looking girl who had just arrived from the country and tell her that they were just leaving a good situation themselves for one that was even better. They then offered to take the innocent girl to their former situation, which was in fact a low-class brothel, where some 'villain was often put into the room' to seduce the girl that very night.[16] One servant girl of eighteen— Case No 684 in the files of the London Female Dormitory, a rescue organisation for young girls—'met a girl near Tottenham Court Road, of whom she inquired where she could get a lodging, and was taken to a woman who kept two notorious houses in W—— Street, New Road. The next evening the woman prevailed upon her to go into the streets.'[17]

Servant girls who had been seduced or dismissed without a character were always at great risk. Another girl—Case No 534 in the same files—came home from Australia after her father died in 1848 and took a job as a nursemaid. 'She succeeded well in service until she took a situation in a private hotel. Here she was induced to leave her situation by a gentleman, and to live with him. As might be expected, he soon deserted her, and she found herself without home, character, or friends—a fallen female.'[18]

Prostitute soliciting a potential client in The New Cut, one of the working-class areas of London, 1845.

Most mistresses were well aware of the fate awaiting girls who were dismissed without a character; indeed, some of the more unscrupulous used the threat as a means of imposing their own will upon their servants. One male servant publicly complained that, day after day, it was the cause of 'many poor servant girls' being 'led into immorality and thrown on to the streets of

London'.[19] Any girl who arrived back late at night was liable to find the doors locked and bolted against her. She wandered the streets, without wages, box or character, until she was accosted by some marauding soldier, sailor or gentleman. Inspector Silas Rendel Anniss, of the Metropolitan police vice squad, who was on special attachment to Plymouth, Devon, told one inquiry how a sixteen-year-old servant had been thrown out late at night, allegedly because she had a bad character. That same night she was found by a police patrol in a brothel at Fore Street, Stonehouse, from which they rescued her.[20]

In some cases, mistresses were justified in their instant dismissals; but in other cases, their actions were unfeeling and their judgements peremptory. Servants with a quick tongue or too much pride were driven from one situation to another, always discontented and never improving, until they could find employment nowhere, so that they were forced onto the streets to keep themselves from starving. Many independent-minded lassies from the Highlands and the Shetlands found themselves in this situation soon after they arrived in Edinburgh as servants. 'There is a lodging house in the Cowgate at the present time', wrote William Tait in 1840, 'where there are no fewer than eight servant girls from the Shetlands alone out of service, on account of their irritable temper. They lodge there for 1s 6d per week, and walk about as sly prostitutes in the evenings, when they receive as much as is necessary for their support during the day.'[21] Some German servant girls, who had been tempted to England by the higher wages, were also inclined to take criticism too seriously, and also ended up on the streets.

The servant industry helped to increase the white-slave traffic on cross-Channel steamers in Victorian times. Girls from France, Germany and other Continental countries were falsely lured to London by promises of better working conditions and higher wages, while some English girls, who knew what domestic service was really like, were persuaded to go over to the Continent by equally dishonest promises that they would be 'dressed in silk, become actresses, and be able to learn languages'.[22] In reality, they were all destined for brothels on opposite sides of the English Channel. If they were under twenty-one, the English girls were provided with false birth certificates to satisfy the official inspectors of Continental brothels; before they left, they were examined by the procuress to ensure that they were free from any venereal disease, and they were inspected again, by a doctor, on their arrival. In the 1870s two of the biggest white-slave traffickers were a couple who went under the name of Mr and Mrs Klyberg; they helped to stock Dutch brothels in the Hague, Amsterdam and Rotterdam with fresh English girls at £12 a time. Many other girls were shipped off to Belgium. One sixteen-year-old housemaid from Brixton 'with an open honest face, and a bright clear complexion, and healthy-looking, like an English cottage girl' was procured in England in 1878. She was taken to Brussels where she was found two years later, by a

The Salvation Army shelter for
women in Whitechapel, 1892.

British official, working in a *maison de débauche* under a false name
and sent back, not unharmed, to her parents in Chepstow,
Monmouthshire.[23]

Estimates of the number of full-time prostitutes in London in
the early years of Queen Victoria's reign varied wildly from a
modest eight thousand to ten thousand (by Richard Mayne, one
of the Commissioners of the Metropolitan Police), to twenty
thousand, fifty thousand, eighty thousand or even more. With
such a clandestine and unregulated trade, there could be no

certainty about numbers as new foreign and native recruits were being added daily to replace those decimated by death or disease. It is equally difficult to state precisely how many of them had once been domestic servants, though it appears that the proportion was very high. The London Female Dormitory admitted 711 women between 1850 and 1856. Of the 157 women and girls with known occupations, 130 had been servants; two, governesses; and another two, charwomen: in all, about 85 per cent. Another London rescue organisation found that about three-quarters of its clients had been domestic servants. (It should be remembered that the proportion of servants in the female working population was also extremely high.) Most of the prostitutes were young. Many in Superintendent Dunlap's division were only twelve to fifteen years of age; of the first thousand patients admitted to Edinburgh Lock Hospital, 662 were aged from fifteen to twenty, and another 42 were under fifteen.[24]

Not all prostitutes were dissatisfied with their lot in life. One former lady's maid, who lost her situation after she had been seduced by a man who then deserted her, had been a prostitute for two years. She was very fond of clothes and enjoyed the opportunity to be able to afford a new bonnet every week; she liked dancing at the Holborn and the Argyll; and her main complaint seems to have been the occasional necessity, when she could not obtain a client in any other way, to parade up and down the Haymarket, which was the most notorious street in London in the 1860s.[25] Two young servants who had just entered a brothel in Plymouth, Devon, co-operated willingly with the owner by going off willingly to Torquay together, and returning faithfully a month later, to evade being captured in an anticipated police raid.[26] There were a number of lazy and licentious girls, with a love of dress and finery, and false hopes of an easy life, who, as William Tait said, were naturally inclined to prostitution.[27]

But probably a much greater number of servant girls were kept in brothels by a mixture of cajolery, threats and force. Clothes, which were usually the young servant's only capital, and her passport to a new situation, were the most commonly used means of forcing girls out on the streets and keeping them at work. Once they had been tricked into entering the brothel, their boxes were withheld for some extortionate charge; or the girl was gradually denuded by being forced to pawn her clothes to pay some inordinate fee for board and lodging. Others fell through drink or force. Some girls were locked in dark cupboards until they succumbed; others were beaten up by their bully-boy or fancy-man.

Most Victorians averted their eyes from all this squalor degrading the centres of their new and ancient cities, and refused even more determinedly to consider the cause. There was a far bigger outcry from well-meaning Liberals and churchmen over the white-slave traffic to Belgium, even though some of the girls were hardened prostitutes before they went, than there was over the more general sexual exploitation of servants. For more than forty years, Gladstone padded almost nightly round the red-light districts of the capital on his self-imposed mission of reclaiming fallen women. He was imitated by a number of Victorian ladies who were, in general, not noted for their altruism, but were prodded into action by the plight of these young girls and the dread of what might befall them if they were left unaided, fears which in some cases doubtless added a quiver of vicarious excitement to the ladies' own more constrained lives.

In 1876 it was estimated that, at any one time, one in ten of all

A Gaming House, another meeting place for prostitutes and gentlemen.

female servants in London were looking for a new situation.[28] Some of them were character-less; others, despairing; many of them poor. The Female Servants' Home Society was established in 1836 to provide temporary board and lodging for servants who were looking for a job, at first, very cheaply, but after 1857, when the society ran into financial difficulties, at the economic price.[29] The Female Aid Society, which was founded in the same year, eventually opened three homes so that servants of different kinds could be segregated to avoid contamination: one home in New Ormond Street, Bedford Row, London, catered for 'young friendless servants of good character'; the second in

Southampton Row accommodated 'respectable servants out a place'; while the third at White Lion Street housed 'the fallen'.[30]

The London Female Dormitory, which worked in close association with the much better-known London by Moonlight Mission, was established in 1850; its aim was 'to afford temporary protection to friendless young women, and to effect the rescue of fallen females.'[31] The Metropolitan Association for Befriending Young Servants (MABYS, for short) was one of the biggest organizations. Not only did it provide lodging houses, but it also had a large staff of voluntary 'lady visitors' to inspect the houses where young 'slaveys' worked, with the mistress's permission, of course. By 1889, it had no less than eight thousand 'slaveys' under its broad wings.

All of this organizational enterprise and effort was admirable, and a tribute to those ladies and gentlemen who took part in it. But the rescue of fallen women, not the reform of the system, remained paramount, so that Gladstone continued to impose his own will and values on his staff of servants at 13 Carlton House Terrace by forbidding any of them to go out after dusk without leave; ordering the area gate to be locked by 7 p.m.; and commanding all of them to attend church at least once every day.[32] Other masters and mistresses continued wilfully to dismiss their servants without a character for any breach of their own arbitrary rules, or none, and to prevent them from ever having the company of a boy friend in the house. It was this incredible selfishness of so many employers which, according to one lady with a more truly Christian conscience, would 'at the last day lay the sin of so many of these poor wanderers at their door.'[33]

New Ways~New Hopes

In 1849 a servant girl wrote home to her brother from Port Adelaide, South Australia: 'I have accepted a situation at £20 per annum so you can tell the servants in your neighbourhood not to stay in England for such wages as from £4 to £8 a year, but come here.'[1] Letters such as these, which were circulated from kitchen to kitchen and from attic to attic in English homes, were the best recruiting agents for the colonies which were then so desperately in need of young women to serve the pioneers who were trying to create a new life for themselves in their chosen countries. Other girls read about the much better prospects overseas in newspapers and magazines, which also published advertisements, giving details of free or assisted passages, while some servants, like the writer of the letter quoted above, were induced to set forth after attending a public meeting on emigration.

Now that Australia is not much more than a quick phone call and a day's flight away, it is difficult to visualize all the discomforts, deprivations and dangers which young servant girls, and other emigrants, had to face on the long sea voyage a century or so ago. The journey took three to four months, at least, according to the state of the sea and the winds, as clippers continued to be used for reasons of economy well into the age of steam, taking out what seamen called a cargo of 'live lumber' and bringing back another of Australian wool. The emigrants lived together in cramped, and often ill-ventilated, quarters below deck, sleeping in wooden bunks and eating from tin plates. Whenever there was a particularly violent storm, they were often battened down below, with all their fears, their sickness and the smells, until danger had passed. Some of the women were usually pregant, so that the passenger lists were often swollen by the time the ships reached port, though these increases were frequently balanced by an equivalent number of deaths among the adult emigrants and their young children.

In the early days, some unscrupulous agents were so keen to gain their commissions that they were willing to give a free passage to almost any girl, even if she was a prostitute or some slut from a slum, if no more suitable candidates presented themselves. Supervision of innocent, respectable girls on the long voyage was so lax that many young servants, like others on the

The caption to this illustration read 'Here and There', a before and after view of an immigrant family.

American route, were frequently 'in a way before they land to become mothers before they are wives'.[2] In 1846 'to ensure the respectability of the single women sent out, and their good conduct on the voyage', South Australia decided to appoint matrons to take charge of them during the journey, an innovation which was soon copied by other colonies.[3] Nevertheless, more than twenty years later, the reputations of the girls on board the *Devonport* were already so besmirched by the time the vessel docked that no Australians wanted to employ any of them as servants.[4] The dangers of shipwreck or of total loss were very real; in addition, many passengers died on the voyage out through illness or disease. In 1851, for instance, one in a hundred women died before they reached New South Wales.[5]

One young woman, who immediately found 'a most excellent

Emigrants had to be well prepared and Victorian manufacturers were ready to fill their needs.

situation' in Victoria, when she arrived there in 1848, wrote home to describe the voyage, which was not exceptional with its many deaths, its violent storms and its 'green and stinking' food. The first Sunday a baby died of 'inflammation'; not long afterwards, when they had just passed through the Bay of Biscay, a married woman died of brain fever, after having been in a delirium for several days. On the day of her funeral, dancing was ordered on deck, 'to chase away fear', the girl supposed. Three weeks later another baby died, and two days after that, yet another baby succumbed, in spite of the doctor's efforts to keep it alive with liberal administrations of wine. (With the prevailing state of medical care, the infantile mortality rate was also very high then on land.)

A fortnight later, they were driven off course towards South America. By that time the drinking water had become so stagnant that 'the smell was enough to turn you sick'. When they were sixty-seven days out from Plymouth, they ran into the first of the three violent storms they encountered on the voyage.

'The sea', she wrote, 'ran mountains high, the sails were torn by the wind, till, by degrees, they were reefed and furled, and not a bit of canvas was seen on the ship. Still we were driven at a furious rate towards America; all was confusion on deck. In the night a tremendous shock was felt, caused by the wheel breaking; the man was near losing his life, being thrown over the wheel, and very much hurt.'

On the following day, the sea was still very rough. Above the ship, albatrosses, with huge still wings outstretched, glided in the storm-flecked skies, while sea water streamed into the berths down below. By the next day, the storm had abated. They set course again and made good speed for a fortnight, until they ran into another storm, when they were 'tossed about unmercifully'.

Dinner is served. Life below deck on an emigrant vessel to Sydney, 1844.

Shortly afterwards, she became ill and had to remain in her bunk for three days, but she was up again in time to see St Paul's Island, which was said to be 'inhabited by cattle, placed there in case vessels driven that way might be destitute for provisions'. After more deaths and more rough seas, they eventually cast anchor, on July 4. It was only when she had finally reached this long-awaited land of freedom and opportunity, that all her

concealed emotions burst forth. 'I shed tears', she wrote, 'at the idea of leaving the vessel, for while in it, I could scarce fancy myself away from home, and I knew the delusion must vanish when I set foot on land.'[6]

The dangers of the voyage were scarcely any less when another servant, Martha, emigrated to Australia nearly forty years later, though steam had reduced the duration of the

Some emigrants whiled away the hours by tracing the progress of the vessel.

journey to a mere nine weeks. The ship she was due to sail in had been 'battered to bits' in a storm, so that she had to travel in another vessel. When they reached the Bay of Biscay, they received the melancholy news from a passing steamer that 'a big emigrant vessel had foundered with all souls aboard some twelve miles ahead'.

Martha's first impressions of both the accommodation and some of her travelling companions were unfavourable. 'We were three decks down and the place was lit by swaying, smelly oil lamps. The bunks were just a couple of iron laths and a ticking stuffed with what might have been seaweed.' There were twelve women in each mess. 'The roughs, and a rough lot they were, were all down nearer the companion. They fought like the dickens. Lowest kind of Irish women, and their language was something to remember, or, better still, forget.' Because of the improvements which had been made by then in the shipboard care of emigrants, the journey was not quite so bad as she had anticipated. The single women, who were cared for by a middle-aged matron, Susan Black, were given better food and accommodation on this voyage than the families; they were kept amused by 'all sorts of games and sports, concerts, theatricals and waxworks'. But their arrival was clouded 'by the news that the best part of Brisbane was under water and we saw a bungalow afloat upside down, a dog kennel with a kitten crying on top, a little dead baby under a bit of muslin, rabbits galore. It made us all feel a little bit down.'[7] Most servants, however, soon found more than adequate recompense for their months-long voyage with all its perils and privations.

The demand for servants in Australia was so high that there were sometimes sixty applicants for each girl. To attract a greater number of unmarried servant girls, some colonies paid the girls' railway fare from London to Plymouth; provided them with bedding; and paid the fare out to Australia, charging them 'literally nothing' for the whole voyage, which cost in all about £20 per head.[8] In the 1860s, both Queensland and South Australia paid the total cost; while Victoria paid the fares but made a small charge for the bedding and utensils needed on the voyage.[9] Some of the colonies had to abandon these schemes later, as South Australia did in August, 1885, in the middle of an economic depression. But these free, or cheap, passages succeeded in attracting many thousands of servant girls to Australia. In the decade from 1878 to 1888, over 21,000 female servants went out to Queensland alone, a total surpassed only by the number of farm workers who emigrated to the same colony.[10] Nevertheless, the demand remained so high, that it could never be wholly satisfied. As the Rev. E M Tomlinson, honorary secretary of the Church of England Emigration Society, said in 1890, the Australians were still 'crying out for domestic servants, and they cannot get enough'.[11]

Some girls elected to stop off even before they reached Australia, as there was always an eager queue of would-be employers waiting at Colombo, Batavia and Thursday Island and, after the Suez Canal had been opened in 1869, at Malta, Port Said and Aden, too. One young woman servant, who disembarked at Thursday Island, off the northern tip of Queensland, eventually amassed a fortune of £15,000 by becoming the owner of five pearl-fishing boats and of the island's

This was the scene which welcomed the immigrant in late Victorian Melbourne.

best hotel.[12] For those who completed the voyage, adequate provision had been made for them to obtain suitable situations. In the early days, some girls had drifted into prostitution through the great temptations which prevailed in the pioneer towns with their great excess of single men. In 1841, Mrs Caroline Chisholm, the wife of an Indian Army officer, established a home and registry office in Sydney and, later, at her own expense, took her first party of girls, who had been frightened by 'foolish stories about blacks and robbers in the bush', up river on a steamer to a district called Hunters River,

where all sixty girls soon found situations at double the wages they could have obtained in Sydney.[13] She went on to establish four more homes and sent many servants out to farmers in the bush. By the 1850s, New South Wales had also set up its own official depot, where servant girls could live in charge of a matron until they were hired.[14] (Both publicans and lodging house keepers were prohibited from hiring single girls for obvious reasons.)

Most of the emigrant girls were general servants. Freed at long last from all the petty pretensions and gross exploitations of England, which bore, perhaps, most heavily on them, they found a freer, fairer, rougher world which offered them much higher wages, better conditions and chances of advantageous marriage galore. 'Australia', wrote the author of an article in the *Victorian Magazine*, London, in 1876, 'offers to the young woman of the working class, high wages, a splendid climate, and greater liberty than she could enjoy at home, either in service or in a workshop, and these high wages can be earned without further qualification than strong health, strong arms, a willing mind and a good character.'[15] In the 1870s general servants could earn from £20 to £26 a year and women cooks could earn up to £40.[16] Governesses, who were in great demand for educating children on isolated sheep stations, could earn even more, up to £80, or even £100 a year. But they had to drop their old-world pretensions to upper-servant status by cleaning their own rooms, lighting their own fires, and washing their own clothes, for, if they had refused, 'those having the means and inclination to engage them, not being able to procure domestic servants, would themselves have become the servants of those employed.'[17]

One governess, Louisa Geoghegan, who went out to Victoria in 1867, didn't like it very much at first, as it was 'such an out of the world place and so monotonous'; but within a year her attitude had altered greatly. 'I am now so reconciled to Australia', she wrote, 'that I was surprised to see by your letter that I had apparently been disappointed at first. At times I feel it is rather dull work never to go beyond the garden or the croquet ground, but then I remember I can rake or hoe in the garden as I please and the freedom to please oneself more than compensates for monotony. Occasionally we have a good deal of riding, and I have a nice horse for my own use. . . . It is a totally different life from what it is at home. In *nearly* every instance you are looked on as the Intellectual Member of the Establishment. You are the constant companion and associate of the Lady, considered—I might say indulged—in every way, and your only difficulty is to civilise the children, which you are supposed to do through example, as they are uncontrolled to a degree, and the parents object to anything else.'[18]

Not unnaturally, perhaps, some uneducated servants, attracted by the higher wages of governesses, made claims to learning which they could not sustain. Mrs Chisholm questioned one of the many applicants, whose main qualification, she discovered

Immigrant girls in Australia received dozens of proposals of marriage from lonely settlers.

later, had been to work as a nurserymaid with five young children in England:

You say you can teach music? — Yes, ma'am.
You thoroughly understand it? — Most certainly.
One of your pupils is nine years old, how long do you think it will take her to get through Cramer's Instruction Book. (A pause) Perhaps you have not seen it? — No, ma'am; but I was very quick myself. I have a good ear for music.
What book did you study from? — I learnt singing and music at the same time.[19]

But the biggest change of all in Australia was in the marriage stakes. From the old world, where seduction ruled and all 'followers' were banned, these young girls entered a very different world, where they were besieged by offers of marriage, if not always from gentlemen, at least from hard-working men who were sincere and often quite well off. Girls who went to Australia did not have to become gold-diggers; they could let gold-diggers propose to them. One girl who was working as a seamstress near Melbourne wrote to her mother in 1852: 'I had an offer a few days after landing from a gold-digger possessed of £600 or £700. Since that, I have had another from a bushman with £900; he has gone to the Diggings again to make plenty of money. That I have not decided on yet. I shall have a handsome house and garden, and all I wish. Dear Mother, I only wish you were here to advise me; the fact is, I have so many chances—a midshipman for one—so you may guess how different things are here if you are respectable.'[20]

If a young girl was not taken in by the first man she met (for there were some bushmen who staked claims to fortunes which had not yet been dug out of the ground), it was very easy for her to make an advantageous marriage. The young servant who arrived in Australia on July 4, 1848, had received three proposals of marriage before the month had run out. Her two predecessors in the same post had both married well. 'One is married to a gentleman', she wrote, 'and keeps a carriage and three servants and gives £20 a year to each. She calls here almost every day.'[21] Even if such a dramatic change in fortune had been possible in England, the former servant would almost certainly have found the front door of the house where she had served firmly closed on any impudent and outrageous expectations of her social acceptability.

Many farmers wrote to Mrs Chisholm asking her to find them a suitable wife; but the only request to which she ever acceded, came from an illiterate, but respectable, farmer who wrote:

I had a wife once, and she was too good for me by the far, and it was God's will, ma'am; but I has a child, ma'am, I wouldn't see a straw touch for the world; the boy's only four years old: and I has a snug fifty-acre farm and a town'lotment, and I has no debts in the world, and one team and four bullocks; and I'se ten head of cattle, and a share in eight hundred sheep.

Mrs Chisholm was so deeply moved by the letter of this 'honest bushman' that she went to her Home early one morning, which was, she knew, 'the *best* time to choose a wife', and after looking at those who were still asleep, and others who were only half dressed, and some who were already cross and irritable, she eventually found one neat, good-looking girl who was happily working at the wash-tub. After she had made inquiries into the girl's character and background, Mrs Chisholm sent her up country to a situation near the widower's home and they were married within the month.[22] Emigration was the quickest, and usually the only way, for a maid to become a mistress.

Opportunities for servants to obtain higher wages and a better life were no smaller in other countries overseas. In the United States, English women servants were 'in as great demand there as dollars'.[23] A survey of servant girls' wages on farms in nineteen different states, conducted by the *New York Daily Times* in 1855, showed that they ranged from 75 cents to two dollars a week at a time when the £ was worth about four dollars and eighty cents.[24] A good cook, however, could earn much more, up to twenty-four dollars a month, or about £60 a year. As in other overseas territories, the new English sumptuary laws did not prevail. One English working-class radical, who had fled to the United States after the final failure of the Chartist movement in 1848, wrote home from Pittsburgh: 'Servant is a word never used here, nor master; you can't tell which are ladys here, the women dress so fine, all of them, and they litterally hoop their fingers with rings an signets.'[25] What a delightful surprise it must have been for these young girls to find, especially in the western states, that they were expected to sit down to meals with the families whom they served and to accompany them to church in their carriage. These were civilized 'obligations' such as they had never known at home. The demand for wives was no less than it was in Australia: one farmer had employed twenty-three servants in eight years, not because he was a bad employer, but because nineteen had married from his house. It was for this reason that emigrants who took their own servants to the States were advised to make them sign a contract before they left to serve for a stipulated period of time.

Wages were generally a little lower in Canada than they were in the United States.[26] In the early days some mistresses tried to maintain old-world distinctions even in the backwoods, so that their maids were not 'admitted to our tables, or placed on an equality with us, excepting at "bees" and such kinds of public meetings.'[27] But many mistresses shared the household chores happily with their servants. As in the United States, the varnishing of floors and the use of a hot-air furnace for heating, obviated tedious scrubbing and the blackleading of countless fireplaces. Servants who lived with Canadian pioneers had to learn some of the skills that only their mothers might have known: sugar-boiling, soap-making, meat-salting, spinning, dyeing, cooking in a bake-kettle or a clay oven.[28] But in the older provinces, there were more sophisticated opportunities. As one girl, from a deprived background, wrote home excitedly from Quebec in 1891: 'I think I shall be one of the best cooks in Canada soon if I goes on much longer, for I can make sponge cakes and jelly cakes, Spanish buns, gingerbreads, ginger snaps and biscuits, jellies, potted meat jellies, tongues, and clean the best turkey and roast it a nice light brown, and also eat it when done.' She was also learning French 'quite fast'.[29]

Although the majority of servants who emigrated were women, some men also decided that they had had enough of all the restrictions of life in service and decided to pack their bags and join the new ladies overseas. The records of the official

Emigrants' Information Office, established in London in 1886, show that in the first year, over 7 per cent who called in person, were female domestic servants, and another 3 per cent were men; of those who gave their occupations in letters of inquiry, 10 per cent were female and 1·6 per cent were men.[30]

A number of men servants wrote to *Sidney's Emigrant's Journal* seeking advice, including the 24-year-old Scottish footman who had despaired of succeeding in service as he lacked both good looks and height. From his letter, however, it is obvious that he had many other talents:

> I have received a pretty good education for a poor man, being rather fond of learning when I could get an opportunity. Have plenty of strength of body, and can do almost any sort of outdoor work; all sorts of farm work; felling timber, roadmaking, draining, digging, and was some time employed as a shepherd, and a short time in a livery stable; have been accustomed to live on almost anything as poor people in Scotland generally are, and have been exposed to all sorts of weather. I am not afraid of any climate. I have a knowledge of land-surveying. I should not mind turning my hand to anything for a time, to get some money to begin with. Is there any opening as waiters or servants in the larger towns of America or Australia? . . . I have saved £100.

Here was the ideal emigrant, and the reply was as encouraging as the footman's talents merited:

> You are sure to get on, go where you will, but as servant or waiter will prefer Australia, where you may rise from man to master, taking service with a rich squatter to whom you would be invaluable, and, when you have doubled or trebled your capital, opening or taking a hotel.[31]

The very qualities which were so detrimental to an English servant—independence, enterprise, and dislike of pretension and routine—were an almost certain guarantee of success elsewhere. It was scarcely surprising that so many thousands of women and men servants should have left their native shores for ever, usually with little, or no, regret to start a new life in the lands of opportunity overseas. Almost alone, they gained some tangible benefit from their long and wearisome apprenticeship in English service.

The Servant Problem

There had long been a servant problem of some kind or another in England as Daniel Defoe showed in *Everybody's Business is Nobody's Business* and Dean Swift demonstrated with biting irony in his *Directions to Servants*. But in the closing years of domestic service there had never been so many indignant and complaining mistresses or so many resentful and demanding servants, like one applicant for a situation who stated: 'I'm not particular, ma'am, but I *must* have scented soap to wash with, and I can only eat delicate puddings.'[1] Confronted with such overwhelming demands from ordinary housemaids, what were poor mistresses to do?

It was little wonder that newspapers published so many articles about the servant problem (usually from the mistress's point of view, though servants did get a look-in, too) and that the problem claimed an increasing number of columns in popular magazines and weekly periodicals. Books were no longer homilies for servants, but had such ominous titles, for mistresses, as: *Mistresses and Maids: A handbook of Domestic Peace* (1904); *First Aid to the Servantless* (1913); *The Servantless Home* (1920); *The Psychology of the Servant Problem* (1925); and *The Domestic Problem, Past, Present and Future* (1925)—if there was going to be any future at all, which many mistresses had already begun to doubt by 1925. The increasing difficulty of obtaining a suitably deferential servant was very bewildering for them, poor things, as more and more girls hung up their caps and aprons, or sent them up in flames as a last gesture of defiance, and went to work in shops, offices or factories instead. For those who remained in service, there were no noticeably great improvements; they could find just as much cause to complain about low wages, poor accommodation, lack of consideration, loss of freedom and depressed status as they always had done. The essential pattern of their lives had been created in the Victorian heyday and it persisted to the very end.

Wages were increased, but not dramatically, barely keeping up at times with inflation, particularly after the First World War, when, as many servants complained, the price of clothes, their one essential expense, had doubled. Mrs Hardcastle of Brighton, Sussex, who kept a meticulous note in a vellum-covered book of every penny she paid out in wages to her servants for a period of sixty-four years, was paying on average only about twice as much in 1928 as she was in 1864. Her cooks got 24 guineas in 1864; £26 to £28 in 1900; and £40 in 1928. Parlourmaids got £18, £22 and £38; while her going rate for under-house- and kitchen-maids (or tweenies as they were called from about the 1880s) was raised from £9 to £18 in the whole 64-year period, which was perhaps the main reason why they left as quickly as they did.[2] In the 1920s, as an old woman, she tended to pay somewhat lower wages than younger mistresses, but even with a few more pounds a year (plus food and accommodation), no servant was going to make a fortune,

The domestic staff of Poplar Farm, Hollesley, displaying tools of their trades. Late nineteenth century.

particularly as no further increases were given once the generally accepted maximum had been reached, however long the servant stayed in the same situation.

Indeed, many mistresses actually made some savings in their hidden wage bill by cutting out the traditional daily ration of beer or money allowance: the practice was already being widely abandoned in the 1890s.[3] Some valets and butlers also found themselves deprived of one of their perquisites, through the concern of some increasingly hard-pressed employers to save a few shillings where they could. One servant wrote in 1894: 'I have been in a great many situations, and I have found the

The staff of Stowupland Hall, Suffolk *c.* 1860. These indoor and outdoor staff display an extraordinary range of Victorian headgear.

masters generally sell their clothes or send them to some charitable institution. I was much amused in one situation with a well-known gentleman who sent up an enormous parcel of old clothes to a well-known wardrobe dealer. . . . This gentleman had the pleasure of receiving an enormous sum of six shillings and sixpence postal order, for this enormous parcel, which I should think was worth at least eight pounds.'[4] The opening of new stores, like the Army and Navy in London, was another financial blow to many servants, as it did not give commissions on orders as the majority of West End tradesmen did. For this reason it attracted an increasing share of household orders from

Mellon Priv.

The Domestic Labour Movement.
Kitchen Debating Society
Charles in the Chair

the families of aristocratic and non-aristocratic officers and from ordinary middle-class civilians who were permitted to use the store later.

There was also little improvement in accommodation, despite some last-minute attempts to brighten servants' bedrooms with bits of chintz and to make the hall or the kitchen more comfortable by putting in a few easy chairs. Elsewhere, barely furnished attics, sunless boxrooms, and basement rooms as hot as furnaces were still considered suitable accommodation. One maid, using the perhaps witty pseudonym of 'One that has raised herself', wrote to the *British Weekly*: 'I slept in the kitchen in my first two places, and three in one bed in another situation, and, when we stood on the bed we could touch the ceiling.' A Kensington parlourmaid complained that servants had to live in dark holes not fit for dogs. 'I've heard the coachman say his horses are better taken care of than us servants', she added.[5]

Complaints about 'bare, cold-looking rooms' continued after the First World War. Miss A Messinger, the author of a prize-winning essay in *Domestic News* wrote: 'In most houses the furniture of the servants' hall consists of one hard wooden chair each and a long table.... A few easy chairs ought to be provided, some books, or something in the way of games, so that the maid would begin to regard the servants' hall as a haven of rest and not have that hatred for it that a convict has for his cell.'[6]

What a hope! Even some butlers were still expected to sleep in windowless rooms between the furnace and the cellars. To get a good night's sleep, one butler who had been favoured with this kind of accommodation used to creep stealthily out of his room after the family had retired and make for the sofa in the coolness of the library.[7] If bedrooms were not as hot as ovens, they could be as damp as dungeons for all some employers cared. In the inter-war years a marquis asked his butler where he stored his precious cartridges. 'In my bedroom,' the butler replied, to which the marquis responded with unthinking spontaneity, 'Oh, it's much too damp in there!'[8]

In new expensive flats which started to be built in fashionable parts of London from the turn of the century, servants were accommodated in rear projections built in such a way that the sunlight never entered and the ventilation was quite inadequate. The *Lancet*, which had a strong social conscience at that time, suggested that medical officers of health should investigate these conditions which caused 'the pale-faced, anaemic appearance sometimes seen in servants in the employment of the better-off class.'[9] But this medical journal's call for a campaign to improve living accommodation for servants came to nothing: it would have been a gross interference with English liberty to breach the sanctity of wealthy homes just to see if servants were well housed.

A servant, in Arnold Bennett's phrase, was still 'a de-humanised drudge', who was often expected, even in the inter-war years, to work for fourteen or sixteen hours a day, with only

A 'Union' meeting below stairs, 1894. The domestic labour movement made little progress in improving conditions for servants.

A lady's maid learning the art of hairdressing, one of the many skills required of female staff.

brief intervals for hastily snatched meals, which were sometimes nothing more than left-overs from the dining-room table; and to be content with one full day off a month, a free evening once a week, a half-day's holiday on Sunday, and a week's vacation every year. Loss of personal freedom and lack of consideration by employers were still the biggest causes of complaint. In 1919, Gertrude Pilsbury wrote: 'We all know that abroad a maid is treated more like one of themselves, why not in England? Ladies thought that after the Armistice there would be shoals of maids. Maids . . . would now return to Domestic Service if only the ladies would treat them with more consideration and take an interest in their welfare.'[10]

This was asking for the impossible, as consideration would have vitiated the whole purpose of service. Servants were meant to serve, instantly, uncomplainingly and unresentfully. The bell was there, so why not ring it? What else were servants being paid for? It was this endless ringing of the bell that servants increasingly resented, particularly when they found after a breathless dash (if they were young or conscientious) through the green baize door, along the corridors of power, and up the long flights of stairs to the room indicated on the call board in the kitchen, that the small task for which they had been summoned could have been much more easily and quickly performed by the caller herself. The curtains had to be drawn; a lamp moved; a smear rubbed off the window pane; a drink poured out. As one servant, with some literary pretensions, complained just before the First World War, 'the successful maid must combine the patience of a Job, the wisdom of a Solomon, the wit of a Sheridan, with the dignified bearing of a princess,' though many mistresses would doubtless have found the 'wit' otiose.[11] The majority of mistresses were quite unconscious that their own excessive demands were unreasonable, though with the human proclivity to see faults more clearly in others, they were often far more adept at discerning imperfections in other mistresses' treatment of their own servants.

Right to the end, the middle classes could offer very little but low wages, long hours, hard work and a bleak future, which was, perhaps, why there was often, in G K Chesterton's words, 'a sort of silence and embarrassment' in their dealings with servants.[12] Aristocrats, on the other hand, could afford to be considerate if they chose, and to offer the helping hand of feudal friendliness. Princess Marie Louise, a grand-daughter of Queen Victoria, who really was a nice lady, wrote: 'Though we had our personal ladies' maids, we were taught how to dress ourselves, to fold our clothes, and to tidy our beds and bathrooms,' duties which would have been far beyond the abilities or inclinations of many self-styled ladies among the middle classes.[13]

Her mother, Princess Christian, also had some sympathy with servants and their problems. Once, during the First World War, the wife of a gamekeeper at Windsor told the princess that their daughter had 'got into trouble,' but her fiancé had been posted to the Western front before they could be married. Without further delay, Princess Christian ordered her car and drove straight up to the War Office to see a great friend of hers, Sir John Cowans, who was then Quartermaster-General. He explained that the soldier was defending a vital sector of the front, but she persisted in her demands that he should be given forty-eight hours' compassionate leave to make an honest woman of his fiancée, a demand which was finally accepted.[14]

Acts of feudal patronage such as these, however sincere in intention, could in reality only highlight the vast differences between servants and their privileged employers; yet, the servant yearning for status was so great, even if it was no more than a lunar reflection from their master's or mistress's refulgence, that the memories of such beneficences were treasured in servants' clubs and halls and discussed for many long years afterwards. (Lack of any real individual purpose often gave an anecdotal quality to servant life.) What servants wanted, above all perhaps, was some increase in status, both in their working life and outside in the world. Other working women—nurses, teachers, 'lady typewriters' as they were originally called, even

How to Settle the Servant Problem

THE OWNER OF THE ELECTRIC VILLA AT HOME

The owner of the Féria Electra Villa at Troyes, whose inventive genius has called this enchanted house into existence, is M. Georgia Knap, a native of Troyes, and author of an important work on the manufacture of motor-cars.

A VISITOR CALLS AND PUSHES THE BELL. THE GATE OPENS, ADMITS THE CALLER, AND SHUTS ITSELF

Visions of the Arabian Nights are conjured up by the enchanted house illustrated on this page—the Féria Electra Villa recently completed at Troyes in France—where electricity has been turned to account in a thousand ingenious ways to replace the domestic servant. Once inside one finds one's self surrounded by the marvels of electricity. In the dining-room no servant ever enters. The centre of the table descends into the kitchen and reappears with each fresh course. The kitchen is run by electricity, which prepares the food, makes the sauces, grinds the coffee, does the cooking, and, after the meal, washes the dishes. In the bedroom, when one goes to bed, the curtains close of themselves and the lights go out, while one has only to touch a button to make the night-table glide towards the bed with breakfast all laid out. Everywhere and in everything electricity replaces the hand of man and conveniences are multiplied a hundredfold. As a *tour de force* in this age of science the Electric Villa is beyond all praise, yet most of us, we imagine, would prefer to rely upon the human agency after all.

SOMEWHAT TO THE ASTONISHMENT OF STRANGERS A MYSTERIOUS VOICE ASKS THEIR BUSINESS THROUGH A MICROPHONE

THE DINING-TABLE DISAPPEARS INTO THE BASEMENT AND REAPPEARS FULLY LAID

IF YOU WANT COFFEE YOU ONLY NEED TO PRESS A BUTTON AND THE COFFEE-POT ARRIVES

HOW IT IS DONE: THE COFFEE IS SENT UP FROM THE KITCHEN BY AN ELECTRIC LIFT

THE KITCHEN, WHERE ALL THE WORK IS DONE BY ELECTRICITY

The kitchen has an electric oven, and all the utensils are washed by electricity, the cooking, serving and washing up being performed by the same agency.

EVEN IN THE BEDROOM THE SERVICE IS PERFORMED BY THE SAME AGENCY

The curtains are closed by electricity, and by the same means breakfast appears on the night-table, which glides towards the bed—and voilà the chocolate.

Electricity as Maid-of-all-Work: The Wonderful Electric House at Troyes

shop assistants—had all secured a more respected place in general society; but the servant, on her rare sorties from her 'prison cell' had to become accustomed to other people saying: 'You do not look in the least like a servant. I should never have taken you for one.' It was even worse when they said nothing. To increase their own sense of self-esteem, young maids invariably referred to each other as 'young ladies', just as the servants of aristocrats borrowed their employer's name to steal some of his social standing.

A rather bizarre attempt to give servants a better place in society was made at the start of Edward VII's reign, when Queen Alexandra tried to set the seal of royal approval on domestic service, by instituting a series of 'Servants' Teas' for ten thousand maids in the capital. After much argument over who should be invited to attend, the maids, in their best caps and aprons, eventually sat down to tea in different parts of London, being served by mistresses who were also suitably attired in their best clothes for this royal occasion. But these alfresco bunfights, which were then such a common means of trying to whip up patriotic fervour or to increase national unity, did nothing to transform drudges into human beings who were treated with consideration.

A more ambitious attempt to raise the status of domestic service was made by a new type of 'lady servant' who first appeared in the 1890s. This new breed of servants consisted of better-educated women, usually of a higher social class, who had fallen on hard times or who had failed to find more suitable employment as an office worker in a market which was still dominated by male clerks. They were more dignified, demanding, and dressed differently, with cuffs of plaited straw to protect the sleeves of their working dresses, and little paper caps which, in the words of one more benevolent mistress, were 'jaunty little affairs that look like a miller's cap in a comic opera'. They expected to be provided with their own sitting rooms, to be paid higher wages, and to be treated with much greater respect and consideration. In these expectations, however, most of them were disappointed. Although many had come from homes which employed servants, they had never anticipated all the needless humiliations and lack of consideration that they would find on the wrong side of the green baize door. One 'lady servant' who worked as a housekeeper for a single lady in a fair-sized house in London, had to do all the work of a general servant in addition to her normal duties, which meant working for seventeen hours a day. Her bread was doled out by the slice and her milk by the drop. 'I am treated and spoken to as if I were a dog', she complained, 'and grumbled and growled at from morning to night. I am hardly ever allowed out, and special permission has to be obtained if I wish to post a letter.' She decided to leave domestic service for good because of 'the inconsiderate behaviour of my employers and the effects of the confined life on my health.'

The need to replace servants with household gadgets produced some bizarre inventions but, as this article says, most people 'would prefer to rely on the human agency after all'.

Another 'lady servant' had been in ten different situations in eleven years and had been forced to give in her notice in seven situations because the mistress lacked consideration. Nevertheless, she had not entirely lost faith in the concept of 'lady servants', believing that a better relationship between mistresses and maids would 'only be restored by a new class of educated and intelligent women, who will raise the work to a high level and prove that the home life of England is worthy of any woman's highest endeavours to restore and preserve.'[15]

Attempts to produce this 'new class of educated and intelligent women' were made at various institutions, including one in Cheltenham, called with *fin de siècle* nostalgia for medievalism, The Guild of Household Dames. At the end of the nineteenth century, Mrs Walter Ward founded the Norland Institute for training a superior type of child nurse who had had some medical training, and at about the same time, Domestic Economy Day Schools were opened at twelve polytechnics and institutes in London. There was even an Association of Trained Charwomen!

But the last thing most mistresses wanted was an educated servant with a mind of her own and ideas above her station, who might even have the sense to demand the latest labour-saving equipment, when the work, in the mistress's view, could be done much more efficiently, and cheaply, by hand. There were even a few mistresses who could claim to speak with some authority on this point, having been down on their hands and knees as an insurance against the possibilities of a servantless future. As Mrs Claude Epps, B.Sc., a former high school headmistress, wrote in an essay entitled appealingly *What Can Women do for the Empire?*: 'I knew one young married woman who had a good staff of servants, but who proudly said she had once, at least, even blackleaded the kitchen grate and scrubbed the kitchen floor, so that she might feel that she could do everything necessary in her own home.'[16]

While they still could, most mistresses preferred to rely on their maids' strong arms. The vast battalions of servants helped to delay the technical improvement of British homes for many years: the middle classes had their cheap labour and the working classes could not afford to buy the new equipment. Gas cookers had been manufactured commercially in the 1850s, but it was another forty or fifty years before a few mistresses started to install them in their kitchens, in addition sometimes to the old range, which continued to be blackleaded and polished. Electricity started to be used for lighting in the 1880s: the first modern power station, using steam-driven turbines, was opened at Deptford to supply parts of London in 1889. Although gas and electric lights were installed in many Edwardian middle-class homes, the pipes and wires often stopped short at the servants' quarters, which continued to be lit by candles, often rationed to one candle per servant every week. Bathrooms were also added to many homes from the 1900s, though many employers,

A more traditional servant problem, the too-attractive maid.
Lady (engaging new housemaid): 'Daphne! That is much too romantic a name with young men in the house. I suppose you would not object to be called by your surname?'
Applicant: 'Oh no, Ma'am! in fact, I'm quite used to it.'
Lady: 'What is your surname?'
Applicant: 'Darling!'

157

This early vacuum cleaner required two housemaids. Most employers considered such labour-saving devices an unnecessary expense.

Much fun was made of the alleged inability of servants to cope with modern equipment. The caption to this cartoon in the series 'The gentle art of training a servant' read: 'Leave her to do things be herself. A gas-stove will save much anxiety and expense.'

particularly men, were reluctant to give up the morning ablution in a hip-bath before a blazing coal fire in the bedroom, so that maids still had to carry the heavy cans of boiling water to the room.

Tea leaves could be put into the trash can, where they belonged, instead of being used for sweeping. The Champion hand-pushed carpet sweeper with a dust-retaining box, was available in the 1870s, and by 1905 the first portable vacuum cleaners had appeared on the market. These huge, cumbersome, hand-driven machines of two-maid power, were soon replaced by smaller models powered by electricity. There were many other labour-saving gadgets such as the 'Do-all', a simple device designed to save the housemaid's knees. It consisted of a zinc tub with two compartments, one for hot water in which the mop was immersed, and the other with a perforated tray where the excess moisture could be squeezed out before the floor was mopped. (It was so effective that it is still used to this day.) Many employers were reluctant to invest in these new household tools. As one report commented in 1944: 'Labour-saving equipment, which could easily have been afforded, was often not bought on the ground that unnecessary drudgery did not matter in the case of servants.'[17]

Servants were too isolated from each other and too defenceless against individual victimisation to unite in demands for better working conditions. Their dependence on employers not only for wages but also for food and accommodation made them

powerless to change the system; they could only pack their box and leave in the hope of obtaining a better situation, or a husband, before the workhouse doors closed on them in old age. Attempts at mutual aid, which had started right at the beginning of Queen Victoria's reign, were not effective. In 1834 a group of London servants had formed The Servants' Institution to provide members with sickness and retirement benefits and to open a registry office so that fewer servants would become 'the dupes of the numerous office-keepers with which London now abounds'.[18] It had no greater success than the Servants' Benevolent Institution, which was founded by William Ashwell

The washing tub paddles and scrubbing board were the only 'labour-saving' devices available to some servants.

in 1843 in the optimistic hope of raising enough money by penny subscriptions from servants, and donations from employers, to build and endow twenty-four almshouses. He was still appealing for funds in 1856, by which time he had left service himself to open a bookshop in Hampstead, London.

In 1891, the dreaded word 'union' was coupled with the name of servant for the first time when a London and Provincial Domestic Servants' union was formed. But any mistress who had fears of finding a picket under her bed at night or a 'chapel' meeting going on in her kitchen, was soon reassured as the union had attracted only a thousand members by 1894. Most of them were men, and so were all twenty-four members of the governing committee. This offence to equal rights, which was even more blatant in this case as the vast majority of servants were women, induced Maria J Sales to form a rival Female Servants' Union in the following year. Unfortunately, but not surprisingly, this union was an even bigger failure: Maria Sales, of Chalet Bellevue, Sydenham, Kent, was not a servant herself, but president of the local branch of the Women's Liberal Association, and a suffragette; the treasurer was Lady Florence Dixie, a daughter of the seventh Marquis of Queensberry; and mistresses were allowed to become members.[19] It was not quite the kind of union that the Trades Union Congress would have welcomed for affiliation. The only organization which did have a partial success was the Domestic Servants' Insurance Society, founded in 1912 as a friendly society for female servants as a result of the new National Insurance Act. By 1915, it had a membership of seventy-five thousand.[20]

There had been a great furore when Lloyd George had included servants in his National Insurance Bill to provide compulsory sickness benefit and medical care. False rumours were circulated that official snoopers would be able to burst into private kitchens to inspect the cook's stamp card; one medical officer of health seriously suggested that licking the stamps might help to spread consumption and diphtheria; and the campaign culminated in a rally at the Albert Hall, London, attended by twenty-thousand people, where men servants joined with their masters in denouncing the Bill to an audience whose passions for English liberty had been previously aroused by patriotic refrains played upon an organ.[21]

It was not really surprising that one man servant, who claimed to speak for a thousand others, should have been willing to speak out against a Bill designed for his own benefit: some upper servants were just as opposed as masters and mistresses, if not more, to the new dawning world of State regulation of social life. Servants were already becoming anachronistic spectres, haunting a slowly fading world where democracy was decried and rank was preserved just as strongly in the servants' hall as at the employer's table. One progressive mistress tentatively suggested to her housekeeper just before the First World War that the servants should be allowed to invite a friend into the hall for one evening every month. The housekeeper, however, told her more liberal mistress that the scheme would never work 'because the upper servants would not like to associate with the friends or relatives of the under servants and would boycott them'.[22] In the closing years, servants became either increasingly snobbish defenders of their simple faith or disillusioned apostates.

The First World War dealt the first major blow to the whole system. Hundreds of thousands of girls and women put away their brooms and feather dusters for the duration to make shells and bullets in munition factories, while others nursed the Tommies wounded in the fight at the front. Some former servants worked on the land and in shops and, after conscription had been introduced, some started to do heavy manual work, such as operating cement mixers or driving cranes, work which had once been thought far beyond the physical capacity of women, though maids, in spite of their feminine appearance, had long been accustomed to carrying cans of boiling water, weighing about 30 pounds, up endless flights of stairs. Women, who were officially classified only as 'substitutes', were soon displaced from many of these jobs by those returning heroes who had managed to survive the senseless slaughter of the trenches; but many never put on their caps and aprons again. By 1921 the total number of women servants in England and Wales had fallen to under a million, though ten years later it had risen to 1,332,324 again, mainly because it was difficult to find jobs in the Depression. (Not all of these were resident, however: an official sample survey in 1931 showed that about 60 per cent, or

This curiously posed photograph of the domestic staff at Freston, Suffolk, was taken in 1897.

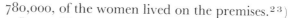

780,000, of the women lived on the premises.[23])

In wealthy homes, staffs continued to be almost as big as ever after the First World War, despite death duties and inflation. One advertisement of 1919 read: Second of three housemaids required, Grafton Street. One Lady, twelve servants in town, fourteen in country.[24]

Many of the high-ranking aristocracy resumed their old ways and liveried footmen were in just as great demand as ever for waiting at table, if no longer for carriage duty. Age had exempted many family retainers from conscription so that aristocratic employers could continue to enjoy their services throughout the war. Writing in 1927, the eighty-year-old dowager Countess of Radnor could boast: 'I have in my household two women and three men, whose combined service reaches the large number of over 140 years! The longest terms of service are those of my steward (Mr Ball) and the driver of my car (Mr Grey). Ball came to us first in Ennismore Gardens as footman; later on he was my husband's valet; and he is now my Steward, having been with the family for over forty years. Grey has been with me for thirty-five years. He was first a coachman, and, after learning how to drive a motor-car, came back as my driver.'[25] But suitable recruits, especially men, were increasingly difficult to find. Even during the depths of the depression, most men were more willing to hawk casefuls of brushes round to suburban housewives, who now had to clean their own villas, rather than suffer the indignities of service, which were sometimes, literally, very painful. One charming lady had the habit of indicating changes of direction to her chauffeur by jabbing the iron tip of her umbrella into the back of his neck.

Staffs of servants in many middle-class homes had been drastically slimmed during the First World War from four or five to one, or even none. In the cause of patriotism and even more through necessity, the drawing room had been shut up for the duration and the furniture draped with dust sheets; the plate and the silver had been locked away; luncheon had been reduced to a single course; families were far more casual about dressing for dinner; rationing brought mistresses much more frequently into their kitchen even if only to ensure that they got their fair shares; and some mistresses actually had to get down on their hands and knees and sample the toil that they had imposed on others for so many years. Not all of the middle classes could resume their old ways after the war and a few had less wish to do so. For the first time in their lives they found that privacy had its compensations: it is not always easy to live with strangers in one's own home, and the interpersonal conflicts are often exacerbated when one is paying and the other paid. In the interwar years it became much easier to live without a resident maid, making do with a 'daily' or a charwoman instead. Labour-saving equipment became cheaper and improved in both range and quality; tinned food which had consisted primarily of meat, soup, salmon and fruit in 1918 was extended in range; and the increasing use of

The coachman's livery was replaced by the chauffeur's outfit by 1911.

contraceptives among the middle classes made it easier for the mother to cope without a nurse.

Nevertheless, in 1931, nearly one in twenty households in England and Wales still continued to employ at least one resident servant.[26] Most professional people and the upper middle classes as a whole continued to have a maid or two or more on the premises; but the Pooters could no longer afford to employ them, though it could have been little real loss to do without a servant who persisted in serving left-over blancmange for breakfast.[27]

Domestic service, however, was still considered of such vital importance that the International Labour Office recommended in 1933 that there should be separate employment exchanges for servants, where officials could interview servants in one room and mistresses in another, presumably to avoid any contamination of the mistress before she had her face-to-face encounter with an approved applicant in the neutral territory of a third room. Officials were advised to make a thorough investigation of the servant's character and of her ability to adapt to the mistress's idiosyncrasies, a lengthy process which made the placing of servants 'one of the most expensive items in the employment exchange service'. In Britain, the government had instructed employment exchanges to set up special sections for employers and servants; but where this was impossible, part of the general counter was reserved for them. Officials had special forms to record any particular customs and habits of the family and any special obligations that they demanded from servants.[28] The State had taken over, free of charge, from the house steward.

The Second World War finally wrenched out the foundations of the whole system by opening out a vision of more genuine emancipation for women. Girls had already lost their sense of deference and were beginning to lose their residual feelings of inferiority as full employment and better education in the post-war years allowed them to claim a more rightful place in society. The last thing that most of them wanted to do was to don a cap and apron again. For a few more years, some remnants of the old world still survived, so that when the present writer moved into a flat in a garden square in Kensington in the 1950s, a kind neighbour, a general's widow, sent in her card and later offered the service of her maids, free of charge, as baby sitters. Nurses with clean white aprons still paraded with their prams in their traditional stamping ground of Kensington Gardens.

In 1946 the National Institute of Houseworkers was set up in a belated attempt to provide fully trained and recognised houseworkers (not servants) with their own distinctive uniforms; but most of the middle classes could no longer afford to employ them. Instead some middle-class 'mums', who felt incapable of coping with the large number of children they had produced,

The Lapsewood Domestic Training Centre in South London offered, 'a thorough training in up-to-date domestic science, three months board and lodging, and a good job and uniform at the end of it.' More than a thousand girls were trained here in the thirties.

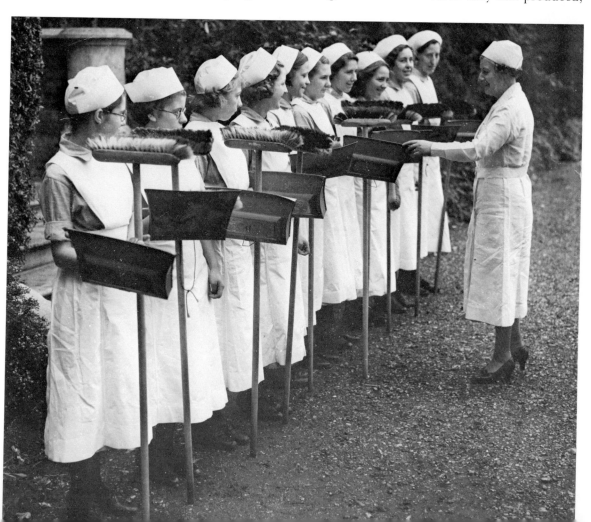

turned eagerly towards *au pairs* as a cheap substitute for a nanny, whom they could no longer afford to employ. In theory, these young Continental girls were supposed to live as a member of the family so that they could polish up their English, while they helped with polishing the furniture and other light household tasks, for which they received about £2 a week and their keep. In fact, some of them were used as household drudges. Some girls were left alone for hours to care for a baby, which scarcely gave them many opportunities for improving their English; others had to do all the heavy household work; others again found themselves in small hotels and boarding houses where they were

The tenantry and household servants of Osborne House paying their last respects at Queen Victoria's funeral in 1901.

expected to work for many hours a day as unpaid chambermaids. Some husbands tried to revive the old *droit de seigneur*. Only a minority were treated in this way; many had a reasonable, if rather dull and monotonous life; and a few had a much better life than they had ever had at home, living in luxurious surroundings, meeting interesting people, and going out to theatres and parties with their employers. One *au pair* told the author that she was even allowed to borrow the family Rolls to do her own shopping.[29]

Increasingly, however, most people in the post-war years have had to do without domestic servants and to rely on the occasional and often fitful attentions of 'Mrs Mopp', though even she will now demand £1 or more an hour, plus fares. Many aristocrats have been forced to sell their stately homes, and others have been reduced to employing a resident Spanish or Greek couple. Even that is expensive enough. At the time of writing a married couple working as a butler-chauffeur and cook-housekeeper would demand, and get, a self-contained cottage or flat, free food, gas and electricity plus about £70 to £80 a week, net. There are now so few people willing to enter service, that the surviving servant agencies sometimes find it difficult to satisfy the relatively small demand for cooks, nannies, maids and butlers.

The old world has vanished, lamented perhaps by some former mistresses but much less so by former maids. Even the physical setting of the past life has been altered radically or obliterated. In those gracious garden squares in London which have escaped the attentions of speculators, a few family residences still survive, but many more houses have been transformed into offices or into bed-sitters. Yet, it was no more than a century ago, as Sir Alfred E Pease recalled, that 'each square had its band, its turn of savoyards, with hurdy-gurdies and marmots, its dancing bears, its barrel-organs and monkeys, its morning visits by troops of donkeys which supplied asses' milk for infants, its Punch and Judy shows, Jacks in the green—and heard the many London cries. . . . The Archbishop of Armagh at No 42 Prince's Garden, went out to parties and to the opera in a great blazoned coach with a wigged footman on a hammercloth, and two gaudy footmen standing behind.'[30] It does not seem so much a century ago but, far more, a different world which we, for good or evil, have forsaken for all time.

Remembrance of Duties Past

Cars have replaced carriages, feather dusters now lie unused with other bric-à-brac on undusted shelves in antique markets, most of the caps and aprons have long since been discarded or allowed to rot, but the memories of domestic servitude still linger on in the minds of women in all parts of the country. Generally they clutch their recollections to themselves, often in the solitude of widowhood; but, from time to time, they respond to their grandchildren's or a writer's requests and purge themselves again of emotions recollected now in a safer and a more distant tranquillity. It was not always so. In times not so long past, when the world of 'upstairs, downstairs' was still a living reality, their just recriminations helped to embitter the female folk consciousness, expanding still further the breach between 'them' and 'us'.

Although few of the former servants whom I have interviewed, or my more numerous correspondents, can reach back in time much further than the turn of the century, the fundamental pattern of domestic service was so uniform from early Victorian times to the outbreak of the Second World War, that their remarks and reminiscences might often have equally well come from the lips or the pens of maidservants who had been born a century earlier. Mrs S Hordle, of Poole, Dorset, recalls in her eighty-third year how she was sent into service in 1905 at the age of thirteen as an under-nurse to three little girls. 'My pay was two shillings weekly', she wrote, 'out of which my father had to pay one shilling weekly for my laundry. The boss was a very nice man, but his wife was a real bitch and treated all her maids like dirt. After two years I had the audacity to ask for a rise and was told that I wasn't worth what she was paying me so I gave a month's notice.'

After taking a temporary post as a tweeny, where she was very happy, she went to a large house near Wokingham, Berkshire, where she had to work 'like a galley slave' from six in the morning until eleven, or later, at night. 'The other four maids', she wrote, 'were elderly and I had to wait on them as well as the cook. I had to take tea and hot water to them by seven o'clock in the morning and the only time I went out was to walk across their park to post the letters at two o'clock each day and to one service at Church on a Sunday.' After she had been employed in

Mrs Susan Hordle in 1908, aged sixteen. She had already been in service for three years.

two other situations, she went as a house parlourmaid to a dentist's wife at Bournemouth, who turned out to be 'another slave driver and very mean with food. In fact, she used to send me to the grocer's for "servants' bacon", sixpence a pound, which consisted of scraps of fat left over from the bacon slicer. She only kept two maids and apart from our evening out, we had no leisure time at all. If she saw us reading or writing a letter, she would bring out some sewing or silver cleaning and she even wanted me to clean the upstairs windows outside. This I refused to do as I was afraid of falling, so I left to get myself another situation.'

One of her last posts was in Winchester, Hants, where the wife was 'another bitch' and the food was practically non-existent, so that like Lady Susan Scraper's daughters she was forced to buy biscuits and pies to 'stop' her hunger. The wife, who had employed thirteen different maids in ten months, used to put coins under the mattresses, rugs and cushions to test her honesty and to slide her hand down the banisters or along the picture rails to see if they had been thoroughly dusted. The First World War gave Mrs Hordle, an intelligent and enterprising woman, an opportunity to escape from the life of service by learning to drive a laundry van.[1]

Other former servants remember similar instances of sweated labour from their youth. When 81-year-old Mrs Ann Wells was still a schoolgirl, she worked part-time in a house at Ryde on the Isle of Wight, going there early in the morning before she went to school to clean the steps and the fireplaces and returning in the afternoon to do the washing up. Her mistress used to give her a bowl of soup which was like water; two slices of brown bread; and a piece of congealed fat from the soup which was so revolting that she used to break it up and throw it down the lavatory.[2] Another former servant, who started work as a house parlour-maid at the end of the First World War, recalls how in her rare moments of rest, she and the cook were expected to 'wash, dry and pick stalks off currants and sultanas for cake-making, and in February, to sit for hours cutting up Seville oranges for marmalade'. Spring cleaning occupied four whole weeks every year, and when the chimney sweep came she had to be up by 4.30 a.m. so that the kitchen and the dining room should contain no trace of his activities by the time the family came down for breakfast.[3] Mrs K Hall, who went to work in a large house in a Dorset village in 1926 at the age of fourteen, still remembers how the flickering shadows cast by the candle used to frighten her as she walked along the corridors at six o'clock in the morning, and the huge sinks in which she washed up endlessly and in which she was also expected to bath.[4]

Hours of work were long and pitiless for both indoor and outdoor staff. One servant recalls how the chauffeur used to keep a bottle of smelling salts concealed in his gauntlet in case he needed reviving, just as, in ages past, running footmen had kept a more exciting stimulant in the silver knobs surmounting their

Ann Wells' sister, Mrs Ruth Douglas, was also in service. In this photograph, taken in 1913, she was thirteen years of age.

long staffs.[5] Servants were often robbed of some of their few precious hours of freedom by being forced to do their normal work before they were allowed to start their day off. One former tweeny, who is now eighty-four years of age, had to help the housemaid with the cleaning, prepare the vegetables for the cook, do the washing up after lunch, and scrub the scullery floor before she could leave the house. By that time it was three o'clock and she had to be back again by six to help the cook![6] Mrs K Rohan, who went into service in 1928, was once deprived of her day off for daring to give the lumps of sugar she had saved from her own ration to a beautiful black horse from a neighbouring farm.[7]

Many mistresses assumed that the payment of a few shillings a week entitled them to take over their maids body and soul. Whenever the bell tolled from the tower of the neighbouring church, Mrs Well's pious mistress used to force her down physically on her knees to pray. One girl was ordered to have her hair cut when she went home on her free half-day. When she returned with her hair still uncut on her mother's orders, the mistress put a cloth round the girl's shoulders and cut her hair so that she looked 'like a monkey up a stick you used to play with in those days'.[8]

Some employers went to extraordinary lengths to crush their servants into anonymity. Mrs B Willcot, who started work as a kitchenmaid in a large house at Bathampton at the age of fifteen just before the First World War, was banished to the scullery every morning after she had scrubbed the kitchen table and laid a pure white cloth, so that she would not be seen by her obese mistress, who was so fat that she could not walk but only waddle, when she came down to write out her daily orders for the cook. The servants, twelve in all, indoors and out, were paid once a month in the mistress's study, but they were not allowed to face her and had to stand behind her chair while she addressed their reflection in a large mirror which stretched from floor to ceiling.[9] This make-believe was preserved into the dying days of service. Christopher Falconer, one of the characters in Ronald Blythe's delightful pageant of village life, *Akenfield*, started work as one of seven gardeners in the local big house in 1942. Sometimes they had to push their barrow a mile through the grounds so that they would not be seen from the house, making him feel 'like somebody with a disease'. At seven in the morning they had to tiptoe on to the terrace of the house and sweep up the leaves silently to avoid disturbing the family's slumbers.[10] Unfortunately German bombers did not show an equivalent consideration for the rest of the nation.

Not all employers were of that ilk. Through the hazardous mists of memory, the minority of good employers shine out like a kindly light. Vicars and their wives, in particular, attract much praise, and there were other employers, usually of a higher social class, whose acts of generosity and consideration are still preserved in the collective memory of some families, having sometimes been passed down through the generations from Victorian times. Margaret Gamble tells me how her grandmother, who was born in London, moved down to Mudeford in the early 1870s as a head parlourmaid to a General Ward who had just built a new house there which is now used as a convalescent home for children. She was married in 1877, a few days after the general's niece, to a local fishmonger. The general not only left the decorations in his drawing room so that it could be used for her reception, but also gave her away at the ceremony in the church.[11] Another former house parlourmaid to a London solicitor recalls how she was always treated as one of the family and given a gold watch for her twenty-first birthday.[12] More than half a century ago, Mrs E Wayman was working as a fourteen-year-old kitchenmaid in the home of Lord Tennyson, the poet's son, at Farringford Park, Freshwater, Isle of Wight, where the poet's desk and the rose arbour in which he used to sit, were still preserved. Although the work was hard, the food was plentiful and good, being exactly the same as that served in the dining room. Once, when she had a whitlow on her thumb, Lady Tennyson called her up to her boudoir so that her own doctor could examine it.[13]

If there had been more employers of this kind, there might have been much greater social harmony, but, from all the evidence, good mistresses seem to have been exceptional. Even when allowance has been made for their smaller number, former employers have been far more reluctant than former servants to write to me about their memories of the past, through feelings, perhaps, of guilt, shame or sheer indifference. Certainly the more intelligent and percipient remain very conscious of the divisions that existed in their own ranks. As one of them put it, there were 'those who were (for want of a better expression) "born to the job" and those who had recently acquired the means to employ servants. *Usually*, it was the latter who didn't really know how to treat them.'[14]

It was the system, far more than individuals, which was at fault, breeding impatience, snobbery and irritability, both upstairs and downstairs, so that if the employer was not a tyrant the cook or the cook-housekeeper often was. No less frequently than mistresses, the cook looms out of the dark passages and ill-lit kitchens of the past as a bad-tempered 'fiend' or a 'tartar'. The butler in the house where Mrs Willcot worked, was so greatly infuriated by one cook that he vowed he would sit her down upon her own hot stove one day.

Domestic service could provide only slender benefits, and far less rarely some affection, in a world of seemingly unbridgeable social and economic differences, where it was necessary for mothers of large families to disperse their young daughters to strangers' houses to lessen the strain on their own inadequate accommodation and slender budgets. It is questionable whether the skills they acquired were ever of much value to them in this century, as they were already anachronistic by the time they had been learnt, and related to a life-style which most of them would never be able to assume. For mistresses, in some ways, there was even less validity, as their roles were already being undermined from the middle of the nineteenth century by the growing campaign of their more progressive sisters for emancipation.

Acknowledgements

I should like to thank the large number of individuals and institutions that have helped me, particularly the Charity Commissioners and the correspondents of various charities; the Church of England Information Office; the Clwyd Record Office; the East Sussex Record Office; the Hampshire Record Office; the London Library; the National Register of Archives, Royal Commission on Historical Manuscripts; the West Sussex Record Office; and the Women's Service Library. In addition, I am grateful to the editors of the *Bath and West Evening Chronicle*; the *Birmingham Evening Mail*; the *Bournemouth Evening Echo*; the *Portsmouth Evening News*; the *West Lancs. Evening Gazette* and the *Worcester Evening News* for publishing a letter seeking information from former servants and mistresses, and to the many men and women who so kindly wrote to me, often at great length, about their experiences, some of whom are named in the final chapter. To my other correspondents and to those who freely gave up much of their time to talk to me I am equally in debt.

FEH

Notes

(Place of publication, London, unless otherwise stated. PP = Parliamentary Papers)

Introduction

1 Aitken, James ed *English Letters of the XVIII Century*, Penguin, Harmondsworth, 1946, p 47
2 Munby, Arthur J *Faithful Servants*, Reeves and Turner, 1891, p 321
3 Sherwood, Mrs *Do Your Own Work*, Houlston's Tract, No 67, London n.d., *passim*
4 Crosland, Mrs Newton *Landmarks of a Literary Life*, Sampson Low, Marston, 1893, p 64
5 Sandford, Mrs John *Female Improvement*, Longman, 1836, p 141
6 *Census of England and Wales*, *General Report*, 1891, HMSO, 1893, p 40
7 *Ibid*, 1901, HMSO, 1904, p 94
8 Milne, John Duguid *Industrial Employment of women in the Middle and Lower Rank*, Longmans, 1870, p 107

Big House

1 Fane, Lady Augusta *Chit-Chat*, Thornton Butterworth, 1926, p 44
2 Quoted in Duke of Portland *Men, Women and Things*, Faber, 1937, pp 30–3
3 Hyde, H Montgomery *A History of Pornography*, New English Library, 1966, p 188
4 *The Education of Henry Adams*, Riverside Press, Massachusetts, Historical Society, 1918, p 181
5 Willis, N P *Pencillings by the Way*, George Virtue, 1844, pp 444–5
6 James, Henry *English Hours*, Heinemann, 1905, p 260
7 *Rambles round Nottingham*, Simpkin Marshall, 1856, Vol 1, pp 100–3
8 Emerson, Ralph Waldo *English Traits*, John Harvard Library, Cambridge, Mass., 1966, p 124
9 Kerr, Robert *The Gentleman's House*, Murray, 1864, pp 246–77
10 Ashburnham MS 2657, East Sussex Record Office, Lewes
11 Tschumi, Gabriel *Royal Chef*, Kimber, 1954, pp 42–3, 50, 69
12 Goodwood Estate Archives, 1096, West Sussex Record Office, Chichester
13 Ashburnham MS 1814, East Sussex Record Office
14 Wynter, Andrew *Our Social Bees*, Second Series, Hardwicke, 1866, pp 274–5
15 Census, 1901, *loc cit*
16 Webster, Thomas *An Encyclopaedia of Domestic Economy*, Longmans, 1844, pp 330–1
17 White, Henry *The Record of My Life*, Cheltenham, 1889, p 59
18 Sedgwick, Miss *Letters from Abroad*, Moxon, 1841, pp 41–2
19 Cooper, J Fenimore *England*, Bentley, 1837, Vol 1, p 188
20 Sidney, Samuel *Sidney's Emigrant's Journal*, Orr, April 5, 1849, p 214
21 Ashburnham MS 2709, East Sussex Record Office
22 A Practical Man, *Duties of a Butler*, Dean, n.d., p 116
23 Cooper, Charles W *Town and Country*, Lovat Dickson, 1937, p 199
24 Portland, *op cit*, p 223
25 Horne, Eric *More Winks*, Laurie, 1932, p 128

26 A Practical Man, *op cit*, p 10

27 *North British Review*, Edinburgh, Vol XX, 1854, p 205

28 Thomas, Albert *Wait and See*, Joseph, 1944, p 33

29 Berkeley, Grantley F *Anecdotes of the Upper Ten Thousand*, Bentley, 1867, Vol 1, p 64

Status Below Stairs

1 British Weekly Commissioners, *Toilers in London*, Hodder and Stoughton, 1889, pp 117–20

2 Fane, *op cit*, p 50

3 Badeau, Adam *Aristocracy in England*, Harper, 1866, p 164

4 An American Lady, *Change for the 'American Notes'*, Wiley, 1843, p 120

5 Bancroft, Elizabeth Davis *Letters from England*, Smith Elder, 1904, pp 45 and 54

6 Greville, Lady Violet *Men-Servants in England*, The National Review, February, 1892, p 814

7 Dana, Richard Henry *Hospitable England in the Seventies*, Murray, 1921, p 75

8 Horne, Eric *What the Butler Winked at*, Laurie, n.d., p 73

9 Wise, Dorothy ed *Diary of William Tayler, Footman*, 1837, St Marylebone Society, 1962, p 62

10 Ashwell, William *Life*, Shaw, n.d., p 7

11 Webster, Augusta *A Housewife's Opinions*, Macmillan, 1879, p 58

12 Thistlethwayte, Mrs *Memoirs of Correspondence of Henry Bathurst*, Bentley, 1853, p 428

13 Goodwood Estate Archives, 1096, West Sussex Record Office

14 Horne, H Oliver *A History of Savings Banks*, Oxford University Press, 1947, pp 27, 94–7

15 Hawthorne, Nathaniel *English Notebooks*, Kegan Paul, 1894, Vol 2, p 439

16 Colton, Calvin *Four Years in Great Britain*, Harper, New York, 1836, p 171

17 Cooper, C W *op cit*, p 185

18 Dana, *op cit*, pp 146–7

19 James, John *The Memoirs of a House Steward*, Bury Holt, 1949, pp 19–20

20 Ashburnham MS 2782, East Sussex Record Office

21 *Servants' Magazine*, 'London Female Mission', May, 1867, pp 97–8

22 Female Servants' Home Society, Annual Report, 1877, p 23

23 Calthorpe Papers 26M 62/F/C1318, Hampshire Record Office, Winchester

Mistresses and Maids

1 Webster, Thomas, *loc cit*

2 Thackeray, William Makepeace *The Book of Snobs*, Smith Elder, n.d., pp 34–5

3 *The Autobiography of Rose Allen*, Longmans, 1847, pp 103–4

4 Pollock, Alice *Portrait of My Victorian Youth*, Johnson, 1971, p 122

5 Hopkins, Ellice *How to Start Preventive Work*, Hatchards, 1884, p 11

6 Ashford, Mary Ann *Life of a Licensed Victualler's Daughter*, Saunders and Otley, 1844, p 49

7 Bailey, John ed *The Diary of Lady Frederick Cavendish*, Murray, 1927, Vol I, p 263, Vol II, p 18, *et seq*

8 Allen, Rose *op cit*, pp 96–9

9 Mackenzie, W B *A Pastoral Address to Female Servants*, Jackson, 1851, 4th ed, p 14

10 *The Excellent Woman, as described in the Book of Proverbs*, Religious Tract Society, n.d.

11 *A Mistress' Counsel; or a Few Words to Servants*, SPCK, n.d., pp 10–51

12 A Mother, *A Few Hints to Nursemaids*, Elliot Stock, 1890, p 8

13 *Hints to Young Women about to Enter Service*, Bosworth, 1855, p 7

14 Mackenzie, *op cit*, p 24

15 'On the Side of the Maids', *Cornhill Magazine*, March 1874, p 304

16 Select Committee on Metropolis Police Office, PP 1837–8, Vol XV, p 104

17 Select Committee on the Police of the Metropolis, PP 1816, Vol V, pp 261–2

18 *The Duties of a Lady's Maid*, Bulcock, 1825, pp 116–18
19 A Member of the Aristocracy, *Manners and Tone of Good Society*, Warne, n.d., pp 162–7
20 *Enquire Within upon Everything*, Houlston, 1899, p 72
21 *Servants' Magazine*, April 1, 1869, p 92
22 Ashford, *op cit*, p 26
23 *Servants' Magazine*, Vol V, 1842, p 58
24 *Ibid*, Sept 2, 1867, p 195
25 *Mistress' Counsel*, *op cit*, p 29
26 *Domestic News*, October 2, 1920
27 Milne, *op cit*, p 199
28 Reports from Assistant Hand Loom Weavers Commissioners, PP 1840, Vol XXX, p 682
29 Ashford, *op cit*, p 40
30 Hardcastle Account Book, Add MSS 5487, East Sussex Record Office
31 Shiffner MS 1455, East Sussex Record Office
32 Cooper, J F *op cit*, Vol III, p 21
33 Logan, Olive 'English Domestics and their Ways', *Lippincott's Magazine*, Philadelphia, 1877, p 760

Up with the Lark!
1 *The Female Instructor; or Young Woman's Companion*, Fisher, 1811, pp 207–8
2 Bailey, *op cit*, Vol 1, p 7
3 Hyde, *op cit*, p 122
4 James, *op cit*, p 119
5 A Lady, *Instructions in Household Matters*, Parker, 1855, p 27
6 Stowe, Harriet Beecher *Sunny Memories of Foreign Lands*, Sampson Low, 1854, Vol 1, p 292
7 A Member of the Aristocracy, *The Servants' Practical Guide*, Warne, n.d., p 46
8 *Ibid*, p 53

At Home
1 Agogos, *Hints on Etiquette and the Usages of Society*, Longmans, 1839, p 33
2 *Manners and Tone*, *op cit*, p 1
3 Bancroft, *op cit*, pp 113–14
4 *Manners and Tone*, *op cit*, pp 30–1
5 Raverat, Gwen, *Period Piece, A Cambridge Childhood*, Faber, 1952, p 119
6 *Enquire Within*, *op cit*, p 297

Dinner is Served!
1 Pollock, *op cit*, p 128
2 Lawton, Mary, *The Queen of Cooks—and Some Kings*, Boni and Liveright, New York, 1925, p 90
3 Hayward, Abraham, *The Art of Dining*, Murray, 1852, p 70
4 *Ibid*, p 17
5 Milner, Viscountess, *My Picture Gallery*, 1886–1901, Murray, 1951, p 80
6 Hayward, *op cit*, p 79
7 Wynter, *op cit*, pp 321–2
8 Acton, Eliza *Modern Cookery for Private Families*, Longman, 1855, p 167
9 Lawton, *op cit*, p 89
10 *Servants' Magazine*, April 1, 1867, p 92
11 Downer, Rose *A Bygone Age*, West Sussex Record Office, MP 937
12 Horn, Pamela *The Rise and Fall of the Victorian Servant*, Gill & Macmillan, Dublin, 1975, p 113
13 *British Weekly*, *op cit*, p 115
14 Low, Sampson Jn *The Charities of London in 1861*, Sampson Low, 1862, p 115
15 Williams, Jane ed *Autobiography of Elizabeth Davis*, Hurst and Blackett, 1857, Vol II, p 60
16 Kittledale, Richard F 'High Life Below Stairs', *Contemporary Review*, Sept 1873, p 560
17 *Manners and Tone*, *op cit*, p 100

18 Quoted in Burnett, John *Plenty and Want*, Penguin, Harmondsworth, 1968, p 225
19 Horne, 'More Winks', *op cit*, pp 31–2

Maids-of-all-Work and Charity

1 *British Weekly*, *op cit*, p 86
2 Collet, Miss *Report on the Money Wages of Indoor Domestic Servants*, PP 1899, Vol XCII, p 15
3 Cooper, J F *op cit*, Vol III, pp 123–4
4 'Maids-of-all-work and Blue Books', *Cornhill Magazine*, Vol XXX, 1874, pp 284–5
5 Report on Education and Training of Pauper Children, PP 1851, Vol XLIX, p 6
6 Garnett, *Fourth Report on the Boarding out of Pauper Children*, Windermere, 1877, p 12
7 Nassau Sr, Mrs *The Effects on Girls of Education at Pauper Schools*, PP 1877, Vol XXV, pp 352–84
8 Select Committee on the Police of the Metropolis, PP 1834, Vol XVI, pp 193–4
9 Collet, *op cit*, p 15
10 Baylis, T Henry *The Rights, Duties and Relations of Domestic Servants, their Masters and Mistresses*, Sampson Low, 1857, p 39
11 Charity Commission Registers, London
12 Cartwright, Julia ed *The Journals of Lady Knightley of Fawsley*, Murray, 1915, p 177
13 Isaac Duckett Charity, 214179, Oct 25, 1889, Charity Commissioners
14 Isaac Duckett Charity, 213717, May 15–28, 1924, Charity Commissioners
15 Low, *op cit*, pp vii–xi
16 Williams, *op cit*, Vol II, p 82
17 Smith, Charles Manby *Curiosities of London Life*, Cash, 1853, pp 144–5
18 Winchester Union Admission and Discharge Book, March 27, 1869–September 29, 1871, Acc: 23M/56/27, Hampshire Record Office, Winchester

Fallen Women

1 Bryant, G E and Baker, G P eds *A Quaker Journal*, Hutchinson, 1934, Vol II, pp 52–4
2 Hemyng, Bracebridge, *Prostitution in London*, in Mayhew, Henry *London Labour and London Poor*, Griffin, Bohn, 1862, Vol IV, p 257
3 Lawton, *op cit*, p 6
4 Ashford, *op cit*, p 45
5 Logan, William *An Exposure*, Gallie and Fleckfield, Glasgow, 1843, 2nd ed, p 12
6 *Memoirs of a Voluptuary*, Kennedy, 1908, Vol II, p 98
7 Hemyng, *op cit*, p 235
8 Tait, William *Magdalenism*, Rickard, Edinburgh, 1840, pp 5, 8, 11, 97, 123
9 Select Committee on the Protection of Young Girls, PP 1881, Vol IX, pp 78–9
10 *British Weekly*, *op cit*, pp 132–3
11 Select Committee on Young Girls, *op cit*, p 91
12 *Ibid*, p 80
13 Talbot, James Beard *The Miseries of Prostitution*, Madden, 1844, p 17
14 *Ibid*, pp 17–18
15 *Servants' Magazine*, Feb 1, 1869, p 31
16 Logan, *op cit*, p 15
17 Eighth Annual Report of the London Female Dormitory, Nisbet, 1856, p 9
18 *Ibid*, p 10
19 A Servant, *How to Improve the Conditions of Domestic Service*, The Eighty Club, n.d., p 4
20 Select Committee on Contagious Diseases, PP 1881, Vol VIII, p 159
21 Tait, *op cit*, pp 85–6

22 Select Committee on Young Girls, *op cit*, p 131

23 *Ibid*, pp 133–4

24 Tait, *op cit*, p 24

25 Hemyng, *op cit*, p 220

26 Select Committee on Contagious Diseases, *op cit*, p 163

27 Tait, *op cit*, p 81 *et seq*

28 The Female Servants' Home, Annual Report for 1876, p 8

29 *Ibid*, Report for 1874, p 8

30 Baylis, *op cit*, p 37 *et seq*

31 London Female Dormitory, Fifth Annual Report, Nisbet, 1856, p 7

32 House rules, 1840–1, Glynne–Gladstone, MSS, St Deinid's Library, Hawarden

33 *Work in Brighton; or Women's Mission to Women*, Hatchards, 1877, p 84

New Ways—New Hopes

1 Sidney, *op cit*, May 24, 1849, p 271

2 Select Committee on Emigrant Ships, PP 1854, Vol XIII, p 121

3 Eighth General Report of the Colonial Land and Emigration Commissioners, PP 1847–8, Vol XXVI, p 8

4 Monk, Una *New Horizons*, HMSO, 1963, p 103

5 Thirteenth General Report of the Colonial Land and Emigration Commissioners, PP 1852–3, Vol XL, p 74

6 Sidney, *op cit*, April 19, 1849, p 227

7 *Memoirs of Martha*, Barker, n.d., pp 2–40

8 Select Committee on Colonisation, PP 1890, Vol XII, p 60

9 *General Hints to Emigrants*, Virtue, 1866, pp 92–6

10 Select Committee on Colonisation, *op cit*, p 483

11 *Ibid*, p 164

12 *British Weekly*, *op cit*, pp 165–6

13 *The Story of the Life of Mrs Chisholm*, Trelawney Saunders, n.d., pp 7–8

14 Fourteenth General Report of the Colonial Land and Emigration Commissioners, PP 1854, Vol XXVIII, pp 162–4

15 'Mistress and Maid', *The Victoria Magazine*, Vol XXVI, p 509

16 Correspondence respecting Emigration, PP 1871, Vol XLVII, p 14

17 Mackenzie, Eneas *The Emigrants' Guide to Australia*, Clarke, Beeton, n.d., p 36

18 Monk, *op cit*, pp 30–1

19 A Matron, *Pictures of Australian Emigrants*, Sidney, *op cit*, pp 22–3

20 Mackenzie, Eneas *op cit*, pp 36–7

21 Sidney, *op cit*, April 19, 1849, *loc cit*

22 Mackenzie, Eneas, *op cit*, pp 16–17

23 *General Hints*, *op cit*, p 46

24 *New York Daily Times*, January 20, 1885, quoted in Foster, Vere, *Work and Wages*, Cash, n.d., p 13 (Appendix)

25 Sidney, *op cit*, March 15, 1849, p 187

26 Foster, *op cit*, p 2

27 *The Backwoods of Canada*, Knight, 1846, p 200

28 *Ibid*, p 137

29 Quoted in Monk, *op cit*, pp 106–7

30 Report on Emigrants' Information Office, PP 1888, Vol LXXI, pp 4–5

31 Sidney, April 5, 1849, *loc cit*

The Servant Problem

1 *British Weekly*, *op cit*, p 123

2 Hardcastle, *op cit*, *passim*

3 Collet, *op cit*, p 29

4 A Servant, *op cit*, pp 15–16

5 *British Weekly*, *op cit*, p 160

6 *Domestic News*, April, 1919

7 Holman-Hunt, Diana, *My Grandmothers and I*, Hamish Hamilton, 1960, p 8

8 Horne, 'What', *op cit*, p 236

9 *The Lancet*, August 19, 1905, p 546
10 *Domestic News*, April, 1919
11 Anderson, Nellie Lockhart, 'A Servant's View of the Servant Problem', *National Review*, March, 1913, p 125
12 Chesterton, G K *Autobiography*, Hutchinson, 1937, p 13
13 Marie Louise, Princess *My Memories of Six Reigns*, Penguin, Harmondsworth, 1960, pp 34–5
14 *Ibid*, p 12
15 *Lady Servants (For and Against)*, Central Bureau for the Employment of Women, n.d., *passim*
16 Epps, Mrs Claude 'What Can Women do for the Empire?' in *Essays in Duty and Discipline*, Cassell, 1911, p 368
17 *Post-War Organisation of Private Domestic Service*, National Conference of Labour Women, n.d., p 18
18 *The Servants' Institution*, Compton and Ritchie, p 1
19 *Female Servants' Union News*, May 5, 1892
20 *Domestic News*, April, 1915
21 Turner, E S *What the Butler Saw*, Joseph, 1962, pp 254–9
22 de Broke, Lady Willoughby 'The Pros and Cons of Domestic Service', *National Review*, November, 1912, p 456
23 Census of England and Wales, 1931, General Report, HMSO 1950, p 152
24 *Domestic News*, November, 1919
25 Radnor, Helen, Countess-Dowager of *From a Great Grandmother's Chair*, Marshall Press, n.d., p 36
26 Census 1931, *loc cit*
27 Grossmith, George and Weedon *The Diary of a Nobody*, Pan Books, 1947, p 87
28 International Labour Office, Employment Exchanges, Geneva, 1933, pp 125–8
29 Personal interviews by author
30 Pease, Sir Alfred E *Elections and Recollections*, Murray, 1932, pp 45–6

Remembrance of Duties Past
1 Hordle, Mrs S, 10 Waterloo House, Waterloo Estate, Poole, Dorset
2 Wells, Mrs Ann, 5 Stanley Road, Cowes, Isle of Wight
3 Davis, Miss C E, 9 Castle Hill, Warwick
4 Hall, Mrs K B, 13 Yateley Close, Leigh Park, Havant, Hants
5 Jenner, Mrs Rosalie M, 10 Claydon Avenue, Milton, Southsea, Hants
6 Hinton, Miss A L, Clyde Cottage, Martins Hill Lane, Burton, West Christchurch, Dorset
7 Rohan, Mrs K, 12A St Clements Road, Boscombe
8 Lee, Mrs Nora C, 38 Topcroft Road, Birmingham 23
9 Willcot, Mrs B, 34 Mendip Gardens, Bath
10 Blythe, Ronald, *Akenfield*, *Portrait of an English Village*, Penguin, Harmondsworth, 1972, pp 118–20
11 Gamble, Margaret, 18 Jumpers Avenue, Christchurch, Dorset
12 Smith, Mrs W M, 53 Cotwell Avenue, Cowplain, Hants
13 Wayman, Mrs E, Northumberland Road, Southsea, Hants
14 Chalman, Muriel, Guessens, 7 Coach Hill, Titchfield, Fareham, Hants

List of Illustrations

Index

(Page numbers in *italic* type indicate illustrations)